Racism in Canada

Vic Satzewich

ISSUES IN CANADA

OXFORD
UNIVERSITY PRESS

8 Sampson Mews, Suite 204, Don Mills, Ontario M3C 0H5
www.oupcanada.com

Oxford University Press is a department of the University of Oxford.
It furthers the University's objective of excellence in research, scholarship,
and education by publishing worldwide in

Oxford   New York
Auckland   Cape Town   Dar es Salaam   Hong Kong   Karachi   Kuala Lumpur   Madrid
Melbourne   Mexico City   Nairobi   New Delhi   Shanghai   Taipei   Toronto

With offices in
Argentina   Austria   Brazil   Chile   Czech Republic   France   Greece
Guatemala   Hungary   Italy   Japan   Poland   Portugal   Singapore
South Korea   Switzerland   Thailand   Turkey   Ukraine   Vietnam

Oxford is a trade mark of Oxford University Press in the UK and in certain other countries

Published in Canada by Oxford University Press

Library and Archives Canada Cataloguing in Publication

Satzewich, Vic
Racism in Canada / Vic Satzewich.

(Issues in Canada)
Includes bibliographical references and index.
ISBN 978-0-19-543066-0

1. Racism—Canada. 2. Canada—Race relations. I. Title.

FC104.S2893 2010   305.80097I   C2009-907442-7

HD9502.C32S495 2010   333.790971   C2010-902057-X

Cover image: iStockphoto / © Don Bayley

Printed and bound in Canada.

1 2 3 4 – 14 13 12 11

For Linda

Contents

Acknowledgments

I would like to thank Lorne Tepperman for inviting me to write a book for this series. Academics usually write for other academics. Sometimes our debates and arguments are inaccessible to those who are not immersed in our subculture and who may not be familiar with the conceptual, theoretical, and methodological issues that we think are important. I appreciate the opportunity Lorne gave me to try to provide a more general audience with an introduction to the kinds of things that sociologists and others say, and argue about, when it comes to studying and analyzing racism. There is much more than can and should be said about racism, and this book has only scratched the surface. Jennie Rubio, Katie Scott, and Sarah Collins at Oxford University Press have been a delight to work with. They have kept me on my toes, forcing me to clarify issues, ideas, arguments, and language. Linda Mahood provided helpful comments on an earlier draft of the manuscript. One of my research projects with my colleague Billy Shaffir forms the basis for some of the discussion in Chapter 5.

Introduction

J.S. Woodsworth, the Superintendent of the Methodist All People's Mission in Winnipeg, published *Strangers within Our Gates* in 1909. Woodsworth was not alone in his realization that Canada required immigrants to prosper as a nation. He was sympathetic to the plight of immigrants, and his book explored the obstacles many faced. But at the same time, Woodsworth warned his readers about mass immigration from people outside Canada's "preferred" countries, which included the United Kingdom, Germany, the Netherlands, and Sweden.

In his book, Woodsworth quoted a "colleague," Dr. Allan McLaughlin, on the subject of untrustworthy foreigners:

The mental processes of these people have an Oriental subtlety. Centuries of subjection, where existence is only possible through intrigue, deceit, and servility, have left their mark, and, through force of habit, they lie most naturally and by preference, and only tell the truth when it will serve their purpose best. Their wits are sharpened by generations of commercial dealing, and their business acumen is marvelous. With all due admiration for the mental qualities and trading skills of these parasites from the near East, it cannot be said that they are anything in the vocations they follow but detrimental and burdensome. These people, in addition, because of their miserable physique and tendency to communicable disease, are a distinct menace, in their crowded, unsanitary quarters, to the health of the community. In their habits of life, their business methods, and their inability to perform labor or become producers, they do not compare favourably even with the Chinese, and the most consoling feature of their coming has been that they form a comparatively small part of our total immigration. (1909 [1972], 139)

"Parasites," "menace," "detrimental," "burdensome": in 1909 discussing immigrants using these terms was not controversial. Even if there were disagreements about where specific groups were placed within the hierarchy of desirable immigrants, the basic belief that some groups of people were racially superior to others was common both among Canada's intellectual elite as well as many in the general population.

Woodsworth and those who shared his views were not thought to be sick, pathological, controversial, or offensive. (In fact, on a personal level, Woodworth was noted for his sensitivity, his concern for the downtrodden, and his keen sense of social justice. Later in his life he helped found the Cooperative Commonwealth Federation, the forerunner of the New Democratic Party, and he was posthumously described as "the saint of Canadian politics" [Porter 1965, 65].) In 1909 Woodsworth and McLaughlin might have admitted to being influenced by "racialist" thinking, but the concept of racism would have been largely unknown to them.

The Oxford English Dictionary traces the first appearance of the word racism to the 1930s. The original definition of the term was "the theory that distinctive human characteristics and abilities were determined by race" (Barkan 1992). When the word racism was coined in the 1930s, what we would now call racist thinking was increasingly described in pejorative terms. Though racism really started to be discredited after World War II, by the 1930s there was already some discomfort with what we would now call racist thinking. "Race" thinking, on the other hand, has been around for much longer, as has the tendency of human groups to make a distinction between "us" and "them." The notion that there was something abhorrent with theories that categorized human value in terms of race or biology crystallized in the aftermath of the Holocaust.

The views reflected by Woodsworth and others would now be called racism. Such attitudes were common throughout North America at the turn of the nineteenth century and persisted within Canadian law and policy circles until the 1960s (if not later). In fact, some commentators have argued that our country's history is essentially a history of racism. Canadian legal historian Constance Backhouse suggests that racism resonated throughout every aspect of Canadian society, including "institutions, intellectual theory, popular culture and law" (Backhouse 1999, 15).

Much has changed in Canada since Woodsworth's time. Racism is now socially unacceptable. To publicly espouse racist beliefs today would be seen as outside the pale of civilized discussion and debate. A public official speaking in these terms would lose credibility and most likely be removed from office.

Another important change is that many of the more overt forms of racism have disappeared from government policies and legal statutes. There are no longer outright restrictions on immigration based on the belief that a given race would be unable to assimilate into Canadian society and/or cause "race relations" problems. Canadian immigration policy contains no official preferences for immigrants of certain presumed ethnic or racial backgrounds, although there are preferences for highly skilled and educated immigrants. Furthermore, there is little (if any) legislation that restricts what immigrants and their descendants can do in Canadian society. In 1912 a law prevented Chinese restaurant and laundry owners in Saskatchewan from hiring white women (Backhouse 1999, 136). Today, such a law would never be able to withstand the Charter of Rights and Freedoms or various provincial and federal human rights codes, let alone public opinion. Canadians now have considerable legal protection from hate speech, discrimination, and unequal treatment.

Moreover, Canadians today are far better educated. We know more about the anthropology, history, and sociology of different peoples. We also know that there is no credible scientific evidence that some groups of people are biologically inferior to others, even if there are debates about the nature of the biological differences that characterize the human population. Canadian values are also different. Many Canadians support our multicultural society that values diversity. Although controversies about whether certain cultural practices are beyond the limits of Canadian diversity are probably inevitable, Canadians generally lean towards a mild form of cultural relativism, in which cultural differences are not laced with value judgements. Generally Canadians get along; ugly cases of violence do occasionally surface, but there are few large-scale and persistent conflicts between different ethnic communities of the kinds that are present elsewhere. We are also relatively distinct insofar as we do not have the same kind of extreme anti-immigrant political parties that exist in other immigrant-accepting countries.

But in spite of these changes, it is still common to hear claims that an individual, an organization, a practice, or a policy is racist. Indeed, rather than decreasing in importance, it sometimes seems like racism is becoming more pronounced in Canadian society. This is true in our media. *Toronto Life* magazine was recently accused of racism by some readers for publishing an article that defined a teenage girl's murder by her father as an "honour killing." Critics felt that this characterization of the girl's death unfairly attached racial meanings to what was really a form of domestic violence. Police forces around the country are accused of racism in their treatment of minority offenders and victims. Similarly, government policies—particularly related to immigration and Aboriginal affairs—are likewise labelled racist. Former Chief of the Assembly of First Nations, Phil Fontaine, recently called the Indian Act a racist piece of legislation that should be abandoned. There are accusations of covert racism with regard to certain Canadian immigration rules. In 2009 the Immigration and Refugee Board was accused of racism for allowing a white South African to claim refugee status in this country on the grounds that whites in South Africa are victims of discrimination and are targeted for unequal treatment. Critics felt that this decision cast the South African government in a negative, racist-hued light.

Despite these claims of racist activity, governments and non-governmental organizations (NGOs) are devoting considerable resources to fight racism. The federal government has recently adopted the National Action Plan against Racism. The fight against racism is part of the official mandate of the National Anti-Racism Council of Canada, the Canadian Race Relations Foundation, and many other local and provincial organizations.

One of the central paradoxes associated with racism in the modern world is that although we condemn it, and although our knowledge of other peoples and cultures improves, racism nevertheless persists. How can we explain this persistence? This book looks at the endurance of racist attitudes and the complex ways these operate in Canadian society in particular, and western society in general. It also explores how racism changes according to social and historical conditions. One of the reasons why racism is hard to eliminate is that it takes on new forms and new expressions as social conditions change. Racism is like the Hydra, the many-headed snake of Greek mythology, whose heads grow back as they are cut off. In addition, there are many subtle distinctions; in Chapter 1 I argue that aspects of what is often labelled racism in Canada are more accurately instances of racialization.

There are of course widely divergent views among researchers, activists, and public intellectuals about the prevalence and significance of racism in Canadian society. Some critics argue that racism is still a fundamental feature of Canadian national identity and that we are prone to a peculiarly Canadian form of racism, known as democratic racism (Henry and Tator 2010). Others see economic apartheid operating in this country that systematically places black people and other racialized minorities at a disadvantage in job competitions; this apartheid influences how such things as income and social mobility (Galabuzi 2006). Canada as a fundamentally and irrevocably racist society is a dystopian view that carries considerable currency in some academic and activist circles.

But others feel that racism is oversold as a social problem (Loney 1998; Kay 2007), claiming that while pockets of racism still no doubt exist in this country, Canadian society is nonetheless a fundamentally fair place; great efforts are made to allow diverse groups to prosper and flourish. The racism that does exit is episodic, sporadic, and, by and large, the exception in an overall fair and equal society. Some go so far as to suggest that the problem of racism is essentially manufactured by a self-interested "anti-racism" lobby. As Jonathan Kay, the managing editor of the *National Post*, claimed after participating in an anti-racism conference in Toronto in 2007, "the anti-racism industry is still chugging, seeking desperately to justify its existence by trumpeting ever more implausible and exotic theories of discrimination." This view carries weight within segments of the political right in this country.

My own view is that neither of these outlooks accurately describes the complexity of racism in Canada. Clearly it exists, but it seems unlikely to me that it is a widespread, invariant and fundamental feature of our society, as so many scholars and activists have argued. On the other hand, it is far more prevalent than those who underplay its significance may believe. Racism needs to be taken seriously. Our understanding of it requires nuance, given its fluid nature and its evolution over time into new forms.

Chapter 1

Defining and Measuring Racism

Proctor and Gamble, one of the world's largest makers of cosmetics and personal care products, recently launched its My Black is Beautiful campaign. The corporation's campaign recalls a slogan from the 1960s, originating from a concern that many black people had internalized a negative attitude toward themselves that black features were less attractive than those of white people. The slogan sought to attach positive meanings to black skin. Some 40 years later, Proctor and Gamble's "manifesto" co-opts the radical politics of the 1960s to sell cosmetics to dark-skinned women.

Another recent campaign is from Stormfront, a Canadian organization advocating "white pride." A posting on the Stormfront.org website encourages members to contribute to a discussion celebrating the accomplishments of the "white race." The initiator of this discussion posted the following statement:

The white race has a magnificent history of achievement. ... I want people to talk about all the positive things that white people have done ...

The goals are:
To enlighten white people about their heritage.
To build up the self esteem of white people. ...
To preserve white culture. ...

Pride is an emotion which recognizes the value and worth of someone or something one is connected to. Recognizing that a family member has done something good is an example of pride. One's race can be seen as an extended family. ...

The anti-white racists try to say that pride is taking credit for what someone else does. This is not what pride is. This is a false definition fabricated by the antis as a means of attacking white people. They don't want white people to recognize the value and worth of themselves and their culture. Their motivation is hatred and bigotry (Stormfront 2009).

What should we make of Proctor and Gamble's sales promotion? And Stormfront's white pride campaign? Many other questions arise from statements that foreground skin colour. My students sometimes ask me if it is acceptable to refer to skin colour or ethnicity in describing another person. The question reflects both discomfort and uncertainty about appearing racist, even in casual speech. (Many authors place words like "race," "black," and "white" in quotation marks to draw attention to their problematic natures.)

These three examples all touch on the issue of race. In Proctor and Gamble and Stormfront's cases, skin colour is a celebrated subject for discussion. In the case of my students' question, race is lurking in the background. Are any, all, or only some of these cases examples of racism?

"Race"

Race is a common term in everyday language: race relations, inter-racial relationships, bi-racial children. Often hidden in certain occasionally prejudicial statements (such as "Asians are good at math" or "black people are better at basketball") is the belief that race is an inherent human characteristic. In other words, we all have a race in the same way that we all have a given height or shoe size.

Sociologists distinguish between ascribed characteristics and achieved characteristics. Achieved refers to aspects of an individual's identity that may change over a person's lifetime, such as education or class status. Ascribed, on the other hand, are characteristics that do not change, like eye colour or height. Is race an ascribed or achieved characteristic? Scientists and sociologists have a clear answer to this question: races of people do not exist in any meaningful biological sense (Garner 2010; Miles 1982). Skin tone may be an ascribed characteristic. Race, however, is an achieved characteristic. In fact, some critics have argued that race is a myth; one thinker has even called it humanity's "most dangerous myth" (Montagu 1964).

One of the well-known markers of presumed race difference is skin colour. Sometimes other physical characteristics—eye shape or hair texture—are also used to demarcate difference. Common sense tells us that these bundles of seemingly obvious physical differences must be racial. But are these more accurately racial differences or individual variation? The answer here is that what is often believed to be a matter of race is in reality a historical social category, created and used by cultures for different reasons at different times (Miles 1982).

But there is no logical or scientific reason to focus only on certain kinds of physical differences like skin pigmentation. Why not instead use foot size or index-finger length as markers of difference? Skin colour may be an obvious, immediately visible characteristic; however, the reality is that it is no more meaningful than another given attribute (Miles 1982). Skin colour does not determine physical or cultural capacities: not all Asians are good at math and not all black people are good at basketball. Skin colour, in effect, is just as arbitrary a category as index-finger length.

To further complicate what many feel are self-evident facts about race is the reality that skin pigmentation is a continuum rather than a clear category. Where do discrete skin colour categories begin and end? At what point does black become brown? Different cultures have different categories. The interpretation of skin pigmentation as a racial category is closely tied to history and politics. For example, during the period of apartheid in South Africa, Japanese businessmen doing business in the country were defined as "honorary whites" and thereby granted certain rights and privileges denied to others. South African authorities endowed businessmen with this status to enable entry into white-only clubs, hotels, restaurants, and bars. It was good for business. In the United States, "black" describes anyone with a hint of African heritage; this is in part why President Obama is called America's first black President (even though his mother was white). However, Brazilians perceive skin colour, and other physical features, quite differently. Here, there are many finer gradations. When Brazilians were asked to describe their skin colour in the 1980 census, they responded with well over one hundred different terms. Furthermore, as darker-skinned Brazilians move up the socio-economic scale, they tend to become redefined as white (Marger 1997, 444).

These examples illustrate that race is a social construction shaped by individual preferences, social convention, history, and politics (Miles and Brown 2003). It is important to recognize, however, that even though there is no biological basis to race, many people believe in its existence, and these beliefs shape opinions and influence social interactions. Some parents are so deeply opposed to so-called inter-racial marriages that they will disown a child who marries outside the family's ethnic group. The belief in race influences behaviour in other ways as well. Landlords may not rent an apartment or employers may not hire an individual because of assumptions attached to race. Even if race as a category is hollow, the belief in it is real.

Social scientists have coined a new, somewhat cumbersome term—"racialization"—to describe the socially constructed nature of race. Racialization refers to how both individuals and societies attach social significance to certain patterns of physical or genetic differences. It also describes how the race label is used to differentiate groups of people and explain certain events in the world (Garner 2010; Miles and Brown 2003; Satzewich 1998b).

It is important to note that a similar kind of argument is used to define the term "ethnicity." Ethnicity is not something we are born with—it too can change. Ethnicity refers to the social construction and definition of groups on the basis of real and imagined cultural criteria. That is to say, societies have selected certain (presumably) collective ways of thinking and behaving as indicators of ethnic differences.

Returning to the questions posed at the beginning of this chapter (Is Proctor and Gamble's My Black is Beautiful campaign racist? Is Stormfront's "white pride" movement racist? How about referring to a friend as black?), it is apparent that all three cases represent processes of racialization. Skin colour is seen, in some way, to be socially significant: blackness is attractive, whiteness is a source of pride, and describing a person's colour matters more than describing his/her height or shoe size. However, I would suggest that the "white pride" expressed by self-described white nationalists goes further than racializing an identity; it does constitute racism. The other two examples do not. What turns the belief in the existence of race, and/or the celebration of one's racialized features, into racism?

Racism

Social scientists disagree about the definition of racism. One common definition, from the *Oxford Dictionary of Sociology*, provides this definition of "racialism/racism":

> Racialism/Racism is the unequal treatment of a population group purely because of its possession of physical or other characteristics socially defined as denoting a particular race. ... Racism is the deterministic belief-system which sustains racialism, linking these characteristics with negatively valued social, psychological, or physical traits.

This definition is a good start, in part because it makes a distinction between racist attitudes and racist-inspired behaviour or treatment. Furthermore it is also useful because it emphasizes the idea of determinacy, and allows for a distinction between racialization and racism. For example, the statement "I don't like black music" is a reflection of racialization, but it is different in kind from a statement like "black people don't produce good music." The latter suggests causality and determinacy; the former may be based on stereotyping and narrow-mindedness, but it does not suggest that there is a necessary causal connection between race and social abilities. Beyond this, social scientists have debated how this definition needs to be made more precise. It is possible to identify some of the key points of debates.

Racism as a scientific doctrine

A starting point is the debate about the origins of racism. Is it a set of ideas propagated by scientists in the late nineteenth and early twentieth centuries to describe and explain patterns of human difference? Or is the average person, with his/her unsystematic thoughts, attitudes, and stereotypes also a racist?

Sociologist Michael Banton argues that the term racism should properly be confined to the world of scientific ideas. He defines racism as the doctrine of racial typology, a body of thought based around a notion of "racial stocks": "a man's behaviour is determined by stable inherited characteristics deriving from separate racial stocks having distinctive attributes and usually considered to stand to one another in relations of superiority and inferiority" (Banton 1970, 18). Racial typology stimulated considerable research throughout nineteenth-century Britain, Europe, and North America. Though scientists did not agree on all the details, the general trend was to explain much of human history and culture in terms of innate biological differences. Furthermore, scientists believed that some so-called races were biologically superior to others. Nineteenth-century anthropologists and biologists tried to measure and quantify everything from skull and brain size to the slant of foreheads, the shape of eyes, and the size and shape of genitalia in order to classify humanity. They then tried to relate these physical variations to mental and cultural capacities among groups. Some scientists, for example, filled skulls with mustard seed or lead shot in order to demonstrate variations in cranial capacity. The science of phrenology divided the brain into different sections and suggested that each section was the source of a different human faculty. This extended to thinking about racial groups: distinct patterns of variation in the size and relationship between these sections were categorized. Regardless of the techniques used, nineteenth- and early twentieth-century European and North American scientists always seemed to arrive at the same conclusion: white people, or Caucasians, were at the top of the racial hierarchy. They differed, however, on how to rank the "lower" groups (Barkan 1992).

This kind of scientific racism reached its zenith in Nazi Germany, where racial science was used to justify the Final Solution, the policy of exterminating Jews. Following World War II, race and racial science fell into disrepute. As awareness grew of the atrocities that had been committed in the name of race, individuals, and organizations began to develop deep reservations about racial thinking and the notion of a racial hierarchy. The period after World War II produced some notable attempts at challenging the doctrine of racial typology. The United Nations Educational, Scientific, and Cultural Organization (UNESCO) played a leading role in challenging scientific racism by sponsoring a series of conferences where the aim was, among other things, to discredit Nazi-style racial ideology.

The scientists involved did not believe that racism could be eliminated simply by popularizing the facts, but it was clear that racism as a scientific concept needed to be challenged. Given the scientific rejection of racial typology, Banton controversially claimed that by the 1970s racism was dead (Banton 1970). The prejudices and hostility that existed at the time, he argued, were better described as ethnocentrism—instances of cultural misunderstanding and chauvinism.

Though Banton is correct to point out that science has largely turned its back on racial typology, it is worth pointing out that some scientists continue to explore racial differences between groups of people. Highly controversial Canadian psychologist Philippe Rushton argues that "orientals, whites and blacks" differ in terms of sexual behaviour. In particular, these three groups show a range of "sexual restraint" and "sexual anatomy." Rushton and Bogaert (1987) argue that black men have larger average penis sizes than white men, who in turn have larger average penis sizes than Asian men. Women of various origins also vary. Black women have larger vaginas and longer clitorises than white women, who in turn have larger vaginas and longer clitorises than Asian women (Rushton and Bogaert 1987, 536). Though Rushton and Bogaert (1987, 543) admit that environmental differences might explain some of the differences in degrees of sexual restraint among the three groups, they argue that the correlation between sexual anatomy and sexual behaviour is likely driven by our biology. In short, black people are less sexually restrained than white people, while Asians are most restrained; these differences in restraint are linked with variations in sexual anatomy. In other work, Rushton argues that black people, white people, and Asians differ in their cranial capacities and brain sizes, which accounts for differences in intelligence (Rushton 1988). As Rushton once stated in an interview with *Rolling Stone* magazine, "Even if you take things like athletic ability or sexuality—not to reinforce stereotypes—it's a trade-off: more brain or more penis" (quoted in Rosen and Lane 1995, 60). Rushton's research and publications have not gone unchallenged. When his work first came to public attention in the late 1980s, his research was widely condemned as unscientific. Geneticist and broadcaster David Suzuki said that his ideas should not be dignified by public debate.

Scientific racism is not the only real racism. Banton's critics argue that simply discrediting the scientific evidence surrounding biologically based races is not enough to put an end to racism. Racism, after all, is not just expressed in laboratories and at academic conferences. It may have originated as a scientific error, but it has taken on a life of its own, filtering down into everyday thinking and behaviour, and also into the operations of some of our social institutions (Rex 1983).

New racism

The search for a definition of racism brings us to British philosopher Martin Barker, who recognizes that the old biologically informed expressions of racism are out of currency in *The New Racism* (1981). However, Barker notes a new trend: negative attitudes toward racial groups are increasingly being masked behind neutral language to appear politically and socially acceptable.

Barker argues that where previous race-related issues had been linked to biological inferiority, a code language evolved, allowing its users to discuss race in apparently neutral terms. Politically neutral language plays on racialized themes in such a way that anti-black and anti-immigrant attitudes are quietly given voice. A 1978 speech by Prime Minister Margaret Thatcher is an example of Barker's new racism:

> If we went on as we are, then by the end of the century there would be 4 million people of the New Commonwealth of Pakistan here. Now that is an awful lot and I think it means that people are really rather afraid that this country might be swamped by people with a different culture. And, you know, the British character has done so much for democracy, for law, and done so much throughout the world, that if there is a fear that it might be swamped, people are going to react and be rather hostile to those coming in. (Quoted in Barker 1981, 15)

These concerns were widespread in Britain at the time, reflecting a fear of large-scale immigration from India, the Caribbean, and Pakistan. Thatcher's speech contains no specific references to biological or racial superiority, but rather points to cultural differences that threaten social stability.

In Barker's view, this language is no less pernicious than the old versions of biological racism, a form of fear-mongering based on supposed differences between groups. The language seems acceptable on the surface, but the underlying sentiment is not.

Barker's book has been influential. He is correct to suggest that the specific meaning and definition of racism can change. One of the problems with his definition, however, is that it is not clear what is actually new about the new racism. Thatcher's speech still drew on racialized difference among peoples, in this case social instead of biological. Racism has arguably always referred to a mix of biological

and cultural arguments; an increased emphasis on cultural difference was not necessarily a new phenomenon.

White racism: The only racism?

Another important issue at stake in the definition of racism is
whether it is an attitude expressed only by white people against
others. One argument insists that only white people can be racist.
For example, American sociologists Joel Feagin, Hernan Vera, and
Pinar Batur (2001) suggest that given their power and privilege,
white Americans are uniquely placed as both beneficiaries and
defenders of racial hierarchies. Members of other communities may
express negative attitudes about white people and even other people
of colour. However, according to Feagin, Vera, and Batur (2001, 3),
"what is often referred to as 'black racism' consists of judgments
made about whites by some black leaders or commentators to the
effect that 'no white people can be trusted' or 'the white man is the
devil.'" Feagin, Vera, and Batur dismiss these ideas as not equivalent
to "modern white racism" on the grounds that American black
people, unlike white people, are largely powerless to act on the
basis of their attitudes; they have little power to deny privileges to
other groups. In summary, these authors argue that in the United
States, "black racism does not exist" (Feagin, Vera, and Batur 2001,
3), given that racism "is more than a matter of individual prejudice
and scattered episodes of discrimination." Moreover,

> there is no black racism because there is no centuries-old system of
> racialized subordination and discrimination designed by African
> Americans to exclude white Americans from full participation in the
> rights, privileges and benefits of this society. (Feagin, Vera, and Batur
> 2001, 3)

By contrast, white racism is "not just individual thoughts but
widely socialized ideologies and omnipresent practices based on
entrenched beliefs of white superiority. ... For centuries now, these
widespread ways of feeling, thinking and acting have been deeply
embedded in a white-centered society—in its culture, major institutions, and everyday rhythms of life" (Feagin, Vera, and Batur, 2001).
Though they are correct to point out that racism has both
individual and institutional dimensions, arguing that racism is the
exclusive domain of white people is problematic. It is not true that

all black people—or people of colour more generally—are powerless in the face of an insurmountable white power structure. People of colour do hold positions of power within the social, economic, and political structures of society. Black people (and of course other people of colour) own businesses, run corporations, make decisions about hiring, and occupy positions of political influence. To claim, as do Feagin, Vera, and Batur (2001), that black people are completely economically and politically powerless assumes that black people form an underclass and that all people of colour occupy disadvantaged, socially marginal positions in society.

Furthermore, people of colour are not uniquely immune to racism or powerless to act on the basis of those beliefs. Arguably, the racism expressed by people of colour against other people is just as socially consequential as white racism directed against black people and other people of colour. Perhaps the best documented example of inter-group racism and associated conflict and hostility comes from Los Angeles. The Los Angeles riots in the 1990s did not have clear racial dividing lines (Feagin, Vera, and Batur 2001, 1). Though Feagin and Vera (2001, 1) argue in the first edition of their book that the conflicts in Los Angeles in 1992 were the result of anger and rage at white racism, there is evidence that they were not just white versus black conflicts. For instance, black and Hispanic rioters purposely targeted Korean-owned businesses, not just enterprises owned by individuals with white privilege. As explained by Johnson, Farrell, and Guinn, in Los Angeles, New York, and other major immigrant-receiving cities in the United States,

> disadvantaged blacks in these communities see the Korean merchants as "foreigners" who are taking advantage of them by charging high prices, by refusing to invest any of the profits they earn either by employing local black residents or otherwise aiding the community, and by being rude and discourteous in their treatment of black customers. On the other hand, many of the stereotypic views that Koreans have of blacks are confirmed in their daily interaction with some of the most disadvantaged residents of inner-city communities. (1999, 406)

The black and Latino attacks against Korean-owned small businesses were rooted in shifting power and economic dynamics in Los Angeles. Latino immigrants were seen by some black people as competitors for jobs in the local labour market. Some black people in the city felt that immigrants and illegal aliens from Mexico and Latin America were contributing to lower wages and taking away "their" jobs. Korean immigrants, who faced different forms of exclusion in American society, had carved out an economic niche for themselves as corner store operators. As major grocery store chains vacate inner-city American neighbourhoods, Korean-owned corner stores fill the gap. Since these corner stores tend to be the only shopping option in many neighbourhoods, they become the focus of conflicts surrounding pricing, the lack of jobs, and other community issues.

The view that only white people can be racist also seems out of touch with global realities. On a broader level, power is certainly unequally distributed, but clearly white people do not hold power in every country around the world. Countries that are not dominated by white people are also dealing with immigration-related tensions. Though we do not often think of China as a country that accepts and admits immigrants, there are small but growing African immigrant communities in some Chinese cities. Africans tend to be involved in facilitating trade between the continent and China. Many Chinese residents in cities where Africans have settled are deeply hostile toward these immigrants. A Nigerian resident of Guangzhou, China, recently described local behaviours: "... you get insults like 'black devil.' On public transport, people hold their noses, and some children run away when they see me in the street." A Chinese taxi driver explained to a *Globe and Mail* correspondent, "Those black devils are into drugs and prostitution. ... They even try to haggle over the fare. I never stop for them. Anyway, I can never understand where they want to go" (Coloma 2010). Clearly, racism seems to be part of the global human condition and not the purview of one nationality, class, or community.

An alternative view

There are many other points of debate about racism, but here are some key features of how this book will use the term.

1. Treating racism as the exclusive preserve of white people is inaccurate;
2. racism is equally not the exclusive preserve of science;
3. racist attitudes draw on varying combinations of physical and cultural characteristics; and

4.   racism is a set of attitudes. As such, these attitudes require two distinguishing features: first, racism must involve a process in which a biological or physical characteristic like skin pigmentation is used to define a group of people as inherently different. In ·other words, racism must begin with a process of what I earlier called racialization. And second, this process of racialization must also involve the negative appraisal of the group defined as racially different, or the group must be defined as posing some kind of threat to another group.

Source: Miles and Brown 2003, 103–4

This definition also raises the possibility that racist attitudes can inform the operation of social institutions such as police forces or government policies. This is why some social scientists also study what is called institutional racism, or the "discriminatory racial practices built into such prominent structures as the political, economic and education systems" (Doob 1996, 6).

These definitions of racism allow us to better understand how racialization is not necessarily the same thing as racism. Positive evaluations of another group are not inherently racist. This is why I suggest that unlike the Proctor and Gamble manifesto, the Stormfront campaign is racist. Stormfront's claimed celebration of "whiteness" is underpinned by the unspoken denigration of those who are non- (or anti-) white.

Measuring Racism

How much racism is there in Canada? Since few people admit to being racist, social scientists have developed indirect ways of measuring racist attitudes.

Social distance and attitudinal surveys

One of the traditional measures of ethnic and racial animosity in a society has been the Social Distance Scale. Sociologist Emory Bogardus at the University of Chicago initially developed this scale in 1925. To help pinpoint a given individual's underlying feelings about people of colour, a range of questions were posed about comfortable degrees of social intimacy. Survey subjects were given a series of ethnic and racial categories and were asked to grade the relationships: as close relatives by marriage, as close personal friends, as neighbours, as co-workers, as citizens of the country, as visitors to the country, and as persons to be excluded from the country (Marger 1997).

In Canada, modified versions of this Social Distance Scale have been developed to examine inter-group preferences, and indirectly, racism. For example, a 1996 study examined how various immigrant and Canadian-born ethnic groups were ranked in terms of "comfort levels" of social interaction with each group. The study found that respondents ranked individuals of British, Italian, French, Jewish, Ukrainian, and German origin with the highest comfort level. It also found that individuals of Sikh, Indo-Pakistani, and Arab origin were ranked lowest (Canada 1991). A more recent Ekos 2000 survey asked Canadians their feelings about individuals from a given country moving into their neighbourhood (quoted in Li 2003). Consistent with earlier studies, this study found that Canadians were more positively disposed to immigration from the United Kingdom and France than from China, Jamaica, and Somalia.

One of the difficulties with survey and social-distance scales is that attitudes and behaviour do not necessarily correspond (Miles and Brown 2003). Polls and social distance scales are affected by social desirability, and an individual may not want to admit that they would feel uncomfortable around a person of another origin. Furthermore, an individual may not admit to feeling a sense of distance or discomfort from a particular group in a social distance-type survey, but their actual behaviour might suggest otherwise. Polls leading up to the 2009 Swiss referendum banning minarets on Mosques predicted that the referendum would fail, but when voting day came, a strong majority of Swiss voted in favour of the ban. This suggested that social desirability shaped responses to polls but this did not reflect actual behaviour when it came to anonymous voting behind a curtain at the ballot box (Traynor 2009). Alternatively, a Canadian in a suburban neighbourhood might feel hostility toward a family from another country moving in next door, but actual behaviour toward the family might be courteous. They may be, as Canadians are sometimes called, "polite racists."

Self-reports

Self-report studies ask individuals if they feel that they have been subject to discriminatory or unequal treatment. Thus rather than asking individuals about their feelings and attitudes toward others, self-reports focus on those who are targets of racism and victims of discrimination.

In its 2003 study *Paying the Price: The Human Cost of Racial Profiling*, the Ontario Human Rights Commission (OHRC) sent information packages to one thousand individuals and organizations across the province asking about their experiences of racial profiling. The aim of the survey was to document the consequences of racial profiling for individuals, families, and communities. The OHRC received over eight hundred submissions, with approximately one-half dealing specifically with racial profiling and its consequences.

One of the problems associated with the kind of research conducted by the OHRC is that since individuals are not randomly selected within a community, the experiences of profiling may not be representative. Those with strong opinions on profiling were more inclined to report their experiences; those with no experience were less so. The studies do not of course claim to be representative, so it is difficult to draw too many conclusions. The criticism of self-report studies is that they find what they are looking for.

Other self-report studies are designed to overcome this kind of selection bias. The Ethnic Diversity Survey conducted in 2002 by Statistics Canada asked Canadians a wide variety of attitudinal and experiential questions pertaining to their identities, and their participation and sense of inclusion into Canadian society. Several questions tapped into whether respondents felt "out of place" in Canada and whether they had experienced discrimination or been treated unfairly over the previous five-year period. Twenty percent of peoples of colour who responded reported that they had "sometimes or often" experienced discrimination, and another 15 percent reported "rarely" experiencing discrimination. Sixty-four percent of people of colour respondents reported that they had experienced no racism in the previous five-year period (Statistics Canada 2003).

There are two other methodological problems with self-report studies. One is that individuals may at times be discriminated against on the basis of their skin colour or perceived race, but may not identify their treatment as being discriminatory. An individual may be denied a job or an opportunity to rent an apartment, but the employer or landlord may be a sufficiently good actor to mask the real reason behind the decision. As a result, self-report studies may lead to an underestimation of the nature and extent of racism in a society.

A second problem is that self-report studies can sometimes inflate the incidence of racism and discrimination. An individual may feel that a decision about hiring, promotion, or housing was made on the basis of his or her presumed race, but the decision may have been made on other grounds. Clearly people attach meanings to how they are treated—sometimes this is derisively called "playing the race card." In some cases interactions with and decisions made by others are interpreted with racial meanings even when there are no racial meanings involved. The question "Where are you from?" is sometimes interpreted as being racist—if a person is not of European origin or appearance they must be from somewhere else, or are less Canadian than white European Canadians. There may be occasions when this question has racist undertones, but in some instances it likely arises from genuine interest. In other words, racialized meanings may be attached to certain interactions even when such meanings are absent.

Statistical under- and over-representation

When it comes to issues such as systemic racism or institutional racism, researchers have examined the relative distributions of individuals in various positions or with different degrees of status. If scarce resources like jobs, wages, and education are not equally distributed, then some suggest that this is prima facie evidence of discrimination that stems from racism. Alternatively, if some groups are concentrated in disadvantaged positions in Canadian society, then this is also attributed to unequal treatment, and may involve racism.

Since John Porter wrote *The Vertical Mosaic: An Analysis of Social Class and Power in Canada* in 1965, social scientists have puzzled over how well different immigrant and ethnic communities succeed in the Canadian labour market. The literature surrounding this question is vast and the debates are complex. However, there are two ways that social scientists have studied inequalities in the labour market. The first approach considers gross, or actual, differences in outcomes (such as earnings, education, and occupation); the second looks at net differences in these outcomes, or differences that remain after statistical correction for other sources of variations in earnings.

Grace-Edward Galabuzi's research in *Canada's Economic Apartheid: The Social Exclusion of Racialized Groups in the New Century* (2006) analyzes gross differences in earnings, income, occupations, and unemployment rates. This research shows that in 2000, the average after-tax income of racialized persons in Canada was $20,627, compared to non-racialized persons, whose average after-tax income was $23,522—a difference of 12.3 percent. The book documents other gaps in the economic conditions of peoples of colour, both immigrants and those born in Canada, compared to white people. Galabuzi explains that there is a consistent pattern of disadvantage in Canada among people of colour that is exasperated by immigration status.

He shows that this pattern persists despite rising levels of educational achievement among peoples of colour both born in Canada and those from abroad. Galabuzi concludes that the educational advantage of racialized groups

> has no significant impact on income attainment, suggesting an x factor responsible for the inability to translate human-capital advantage into wages and occupational status. We suggest that the x factor is the devaluation of the human capital of racialized group members, resulting from racial discrimination in the labour market. (Galabuzi 2006, 111)

Galabuzi sees a new "colour-coded" vertical mosaic in Canada.

The under-representation of minorities in certain prestigious positions, such as Canadian university presidents, has been examined by Reza Nakhaie; this research reveals that peoples of colour are under-represented among senior university administrators, and he argues that this overall pattern of under-representation "justifies various charges of racism directed at Canadian universities" (Nakhaie 2004, 100).

Other research tries to further untangle Galabuzi's X factor, introducing new control measures and exploring other possible factors. This "net approach" provides a more sophisticated understanding of these differences. Clearly, an individual's level of earnings in Canadian society depends on a number of variables: middle-aged workers earn more than young workers, men earn more than women, higher levels of education result in higher earnings, working full time versus part time makes a difference in earnings.

There are a range of structural factors, including geographical area of residence, occupation, and industry of employment. Researchers use the net approach to compare group outcomes after these other sources of variation are statistically taken into account. As other sources of variation in earnings are ruled out, greater confidence can be placed in the conclusion that the X factor really is racist discrimination.

Research using the net approach presents a much more complicated picture of the nature of inequality in Canada. Being born in Canada makes a big difference for most groups, and so does gender. The research also shows that not all people of colour are at a disadvantage, but the one group that consistently lags behind others is black men (Hum and Simpson 2007). This nuanced understanding is more helpful than the blanket characterization of a uniformly racialized system of inequality in Canada.

Racism as ideology and discourse

As we saw earlier in this chapter, some social scientists define racism as a form of ideology and measure that ideology by examining social discourses. France Henry and Carol Tator are perhaps the most thoughtful and influential proponents of this approach.

Henry and Tator explore the extent of negative feelings directed against racialized groups in Canada, as well as differential treatment and institutionalized discrimination. They argue that democratic racism is a way for Canadians to unconsciously rationalize racial disadvantage in order to maintain the belief that Canada is a fundamentally fair society. Democratic racism, they believe, needs to be measured through the exertion of dominance and the effects such racism has on society.

For example, Henry and Tator argue that the idea of multiculturalism is racist insofar as it promotes tolerance, accommodation, sensitivity, harmony, and diversity. These concepts, however, do not reflect openness and fairness, or genuine respect for and the social recognition of racialized groups. Rather, they indirectly promote the notion that "the dominant way is superior." The ideology of multiculturalism inherently implies that there is a ceiling on tolerance and diversity. Henry and Tator argue that "declarations of the need for tolerance and harmony tend to conceal the messy business of structural and systemic inequality and the unequal relations of power that continue to exist within a democratic liberal society." Rather than being a recipe for inter-group harmony, those who support multicultural policies as the solution to inter-group tensions and inequalities are not only deluding themselves, they are in fact democratic racists in their inability (or refusal) to recognize the structural basis to racism and discrimination.

This approach is influential and has merit, but it is also an overly broad measure of racism. It includes a wide variety of beliefs and attitudes treated as examples of racism. Moreover, this analysis leaves the impression that any *idea* that questions the seemingly fundamental and widespread existence of racism in the country is a form of racism. It also assumes that racism can be measured independently of individuals' motives and intentions, and independently of the context within which people believe certain things about the world. In other words, certain ideas, ideologies, and discourses are inherently racist, regardless of the context and motives underlying those ideas.

In sum, this definition of racism is deeply problematic. In Henry and Tator's approach, the analytical task of measuring racism ultimately involves determining how willingly a given theory accepts that racism is a fundamental aspect of Canadian society. But insisting that any theory that fails to see racism at work throughout the country is ultimately too low of a bar to usefully measure the scope of racism.

Racism is tricky to define and to measure. Social scientists seeking to quantify racism in this country face a number of challenges. Social desirability comes into play, as does the fact that racism is a term of political abuse. There is no single perfect measure of racism. Each of the definitions and measures described in this chapter contributes to pieces of a puzzle, but the overall picture remains unclear. Is Canadian society rife with racism, or is racism episodic, specific, nuanced, and always operating in different ways? The remaining chapters explore this question further by examining specific issues related to immigration, Aboriginal relations, and the experiences of black people and Muslims in Canada.

Chapter 2

Explaining Racism

Explanations of racism focus on a wide variety of topics. Is it a natural human tendency or a psychological disorder? Do people make rational calculations and choices when they discriminate against individuals or groups? Is racism a product of our environment and the ways we are socialized by our family, friends, and the media?

Psychology

Firoz Khan, a Vancouver delivery truck driver, was assaulted by three off-duty police officers in 2009. One of the officers was reported to have said "we don't like brown people" (Rolfson and Hill 2009) before he started kicking and punching Mr. Khan on a street in downtown Vancouver.

Psychological models explore how prejudice—an unfavourable, generalized, and rigid belief directed toward all members of a group—and racism satisfy certain emotional or personal needs of individuals. There are many variations of psychological explanations (all of which cannot be reviewed here). *Frustration-aggression* explains prejudice and racism as forms of hostility that arise from individual frustration. The theory suggests that people who are dissatisfied with their circumstances—such as a low-paying job, rejection from a university program, or not making a sports team— respond with aggression (Marger 1997). Since the real source of frustration is usually too powerful to confront directly (or may be unknown), people take out their dissatisfaction on others less powerful than themselves. Ethnic and racial groups are convenient and safe targets of displaced aggression, otherwise known as scapegoats. Frustration-aggression is sometimes used to explain anti-Semitism—negative attitudes and everyday discrimination directed against Jews (Brym and Lenton 1993).

Another model sees racism as an expression of an *authoritarian personality*. This model was advanced after World War II to explain the rise of Nazism in Germany; it holds that prejudice, along with participation in extremist political movements, is the result of a particular personality type. The authoritarian personality involves certain characteristics including conformity, discipline, cynicism, intolerance, and a preoccupation with power (Marger 1997, 95). These personality traits spill over into other aspects of a person's life, including child rearing, political support, religious beliefs, and job choice.

Psychological models compellingly frame racism as an individual problem. We all have bad days at work or at school, and we may lash out at the people close to us. The full story of the off-duty police officers' assault on Firoz Khan has yet to come out, but drawing on the frustration-aggression model it is possible to conjecture that the three officers attacked as a result of frustration in other areas of their lives. Alternatively, the authoritarian personality model might suggest that police work attracts individuals who have authoritarian tendencies. The police are, after all, a military organization where rank, authority, and obedience are required. Perhaps it was the officers' personality type that made them lash out at Mr. Khan.

Models that explain racism as a matter of individual pathology have limitations. First, people respond to frustrating circumstances in a variety of ways. The frustration-aggression model does not explain a given response to frustrating circumstances. Some people internalize frustrations and others develop creative solutions. Second, these models fail to explain why certain groups are chosen as scapegoats. Third, there is no room for context in these models: they fail to recognize that prejudice is a product of "situations, historical situations, economic situations, political situations; it is not a little demon that emerges in people simply because they are depraved" (Schermerhorn 1970, 6, quoted in Marger 1997, 92).

Sociobiology

Is racism an inevitable consequence of visibly different groups of people coming into contact with each other as a result of mass migration? Sociobiologists argue that prejudice and discrimination stem from our supposedly biologically grounded tendency to be nepotistic. In other words, the process of natural selection does not operate among individuals, but rather at the level of kin-related groups. Clusters of genes, they argue, are passed-on through what they call kin selection (Wilson 1978).

Here, ethnic and racial groups are envisioned as large extended families. Since people have a "natural" tendency to want to pass on their genes, they favour their own families. Thus people are inherently both altruistic (prepared to sacrifice their own individual interests for the sake of the group) and ethnocentric. Humans, therefore, have a natural distrust and dislike of non-family members (van den Berghe 1986, 255). Ethnicity and race serve as clues to, or markers of, genetic closeness.

Sociobiologists argue that racism can be expected to arise "whenever variance in inherited physical appearance is greater between groups than within groups" as a consequence of long-distance migration (van den Berghe 1995, 362). Racism became particularly widespread in the late nineteenth and early twentieth centuries as a result of large-scale, international migration. In van den Berghe's view, skin colour is the "reliable, easy and fast" way of recognizing genetically related kin. This is also why "Norwegians and Swedes could never be racists toward one another, even if they wanted to," as they cannot easily distinguish themselves.

Are racism, prejudice, and discrimination programmed into us by our genes? It seems unlikely. One of the problems with the sociobiological explanation of racism is that it doesn't account for conflict within an ethnic group. In the history of the United States, white workers have struck against white-owned factories, and Americans have killed members of their own ethnic or racial group without concern for race (Bonacich 1980). Another problem is that sociobiology does not explain how and why we frequently break out of our supposed genetically programmed nepotism. For example, Canadians of diverse backgrounds participate together in various kinds of anti-racist social movements (Henry and Tator 2010). Ethnic and race relations, therefore, are not necessarily zero-sum games in which one group wins at the expense of another. Another flaw with this argument is that if racism is the inevitable result of long-distance migration, Canada should be one of the most racist places on earth. Given the dramatic increase of immigration in Canada in the 1980s and 1990s, this theory would predict more inter-group tension. But this is not the case; Canadians are far less racist than they were one hundred years ago.

The Importance of Socialization

Normative theories of ethnic and racial prejudices concentrate on the ways in which both identities and prejudices are transmitted through socialization and the social circumstances that underpin discriminatory behaviour (Marger 1997). These theories consider how social norms and group pressures form attitudes and identities. One area of socialization studies focuses on how we are taught ethnic and racial stereotypes, prejudices, and attitudes by our families, peer groups, and the mass media. Dionne Brand and Krisantha Sri Bhaggiyadatta (2003, 277) explain that socialization for children can begin as early as daycare or on the playground.

Another focus of the socialization approach is the ways in which ethnic and racial identities are constructed and maintained. We saw in Chapter 1 that race is not an ascribed characteristic, but rather a socially constructed category. This is also true of ethnicities, which change over the course of generations. Being Ukrainian does not mean the same thing for recent immigrants from Ukraine as it does for the children and grandchildren of those immigrants. Being fluent in Ukrainian is less important for second and third generations. The children of immigrants tend to become more interested in the symbolic aspects of the culture of their parents, such as foodways and cultural practices. They are also more likely to develop joint identities: Ukranian Canadian.

Social scientists who study socialization also explore how individuals and groups identify with a given group, and the social consequences of these attachments. Socialization theories are superior to psychological and sociobiological approaches in their emphasis on how attitudes are learned through social interaction. The limitation of socialization theories is that they are unable to explain how prejudicial ideas, attitudes, and practices arise in the first place.

Racism as a Rational Choice

Consider the following example of discriminatory behaviour in Britain:

Most students coming to London University [in England] during the years following World War II had to find lodgings in private houses. Black- and brown-skinned students discovered that if they were to secure accommodation of the same quality as that secured by White students, they had to pay more—either because there were charged a higher rent or because, to find comparable accommodation, they had to travel farther afield and incur higher travel costs. This extra premium that they had to pay was called a "color tax." ... The darker-skinned a student was, the higher the tax was likely to be. (Banton 1995, 478)

Were the white British landlords who were renting flats at selectively higher prices "authoritarian personalities"? Were they engaging in scapegoating? By asking for lower rents from white students, were they expressing a sociobiological preference toward their perceived white kin? The first two explanations fail to convince. The latter is problematic: it would be impossible to disprove that discriminatory behaviour is rooted in nepotism. In other words, sociobiology claims to explain an enormous range of possible behaviours via the same process.

Some social scientists see racism as a rational choice. In the same way that people make choices about where to live or how much education to acquire, individuals make choices about whether to discriminate and treat others unequally. Rational choice approaches to race and ethnic relations start from the basic assumption that "individuals act so as to obtain maximum net advantage" (Banton 1995, 479). Individuals weigh the costs and benefits associated with different courses of action, and generally choose whatever will maximize benefits and minimize costs (recall the South African government that made the Japanese business professionals "honorary whites").

How would this approach explain the "colour tax" that white landlords made on certain groups of students in the postwar period? According to Michael Banton, in the context of postwar London, many of the individuals looking to rent out rooms were middle-aged widows, or women who had inherited their homes. They were renting rooms from economic necessity. They usually provided meals; sometimes they washed their lodger's clothing, and sometimes they had strict curfews and rules about visits by guests of the opposite sex. Their reluctance to rent rooms to African and Indian students studying at the University of London was rooted in a fear that interpersonal relationships with these students might be more difficult and challenging (they might not know what kind of food to make; they might have found it hard to understand their accents), and they feared that their own status would be diminished in the eyes of their neighbours. If they took in African and Indian students, they feared that their neighbours might think that the reason they did not take in white students was that the standard of their rooms was low, the rooms were not clean enough, or they were poor cooks. The colour tax had become a kind of additional compensation to cover the landlords' perceived loss of status in the eyes of their neighbours.

This kind of explanation has also been used to explain collective behaviours like ethnic nationalism and ethnic cleansing, as well as social phenomena such as Hutterites and Amish communities that intentionally reject some aspects of modernity. For example, the conflicts in the former Yugoslavia in the 1990s have been explained as the result of rational choices made by different groups of people:

> It is not difficult to interpret events as the by-product of a cool, calculating land grab by Serbs and Croats against their weaker Muslim victims, for grabbing land, like other forms of looting, is profitable in the absence of effective state authority. (Hechter 1995, 54, quoted in Malešević 2002, 203)

Groups like Hutterites can maintain themselves in a modernized world by what rational choice theorists call "raising the exit costs," or costs of leaving the group. They do this by controlling education, which helps shape their children's preferences for group-related activities, and by limiting the development of skills that would allow their children to make it in the outside world.

Racism, Power, and Conflict

This model sees racism as being connected to power relations and to social conflict. Political economists see societies as being fundamentally conflict-ridden, with different groups fighting over scarce resources like jobs, incomes, housing, power, and prestige. Here, racism is linked to efforts on the part of one group to maintain positions of power and privilege over other groups.

Political economists argue that people do not dislike each other simply because of skin colour; rather, in situations of conflict, racial and ethnic symbols are used to represent some other "more fundamental reality" (Bonacich 1979, 19). Political economists have argued that "race problems begin as labour problems" (Bolaria and Li 1988, 7), where contacts between different groups do not occur through the innocent or neutral mixing of populations. Unlike sociobiologists who argue that the reasons for migration are largely unimportant in explaining conflict, political economists see different groups interacting out of economic imperatives associated with trade, colonization, migration, and the search for production sites and labour power. Groups coming into contact for economic reasons are a key part of the basis for racial hostility and racism.

Some early versions of political economy focused on the specific issue of racism and slavery. Slavery emerged not because of beliefs in a superior white race and inferior black race, but rather because plantation owners needed cheap labour. The construction of racial ideologies justified treating one group of people—Africans—as a source of forced labour. According to American sociologist Oliver Cromwell Cox:

> Sometimes, probably because of its very obviousness, it is not real-
> ized that the slave trade was simply a way of recruiting labour for
> the purpose of exploiting the great natural resources of America. This
> trade did not develop because Indians and Negroes were red and black
> ... but because they were the best workers to be found for the heavy
> labour in the mines and plantations across the Atlantic. (1948, 23)

For plantation owners and slave traders in search of ever-cheaper sources of labour, racism was used to dehumanize Africans, justifying their exploitation. Hence the argument in this model that defining some groups of people as biologically inferior is a useful justification for poor pay and poor treatment.

Ashley Montagu (1964), in a slightly different version of this argument, contends that racism emerged just as serious moral and ethical questions were being raised about slavery—when calls for the abolition of slavery were arising. According to Montagu:

> It was only when voices began to make themselves heard against the
> inhuman traffic in slaves, and when these voices assumed the shape of

influential men and organizations, that, on the defensive, the supporters of slavery were forced to look about them for reasons of a new kind
to controvert the dangerous arguments of their opponents. (1964, 39)

Supporters of slavery, according to Montagu, latched onto the idea
of race; they promoted the belief that black people and white people
were inherently different in their mental and physical capacities and
that the former were inferior. "[T]he idea of race was, in fact, the
deliberate creation of an exploiting class which was seeking to maintain and defend its privileges against what was profitably regarded as
an inferior social caste" (Montagu 1964, 50).

Racism did not end with the demise of slavery, and political economists use broadly similar arguments to explain more modern forms
of racism. It has been argued that racism was employed as a weapon
in the super-exploitation of certain groups of workers and as a
strategy developed by employers to divide and conquer the working
class (Castles and Kosack 1973). Racist theories were propagated
by capitalists in the nineteenth and twentieth centuries as a way of
creating artificial distinctions between different groups of workers. By
perpetuating ideas about racial superiority and inferiority, capitalists
were able to sow discontent within the working class, reduce the
unity of workers, and so better control them. Racism, according to
this approach, deflects workers' attention away from the true source
of their socio-economic problems—the capitalist system—and
instead encourages them to focus on each other as the source of their
problems:

> Race provides a convenient basis for generating low-cost labour, and
> racial discrimination serves as an effective barrier in preventing non-
> white workers from moving away from undesirable jobs. ... Advanced
> capitalist countries rely on immigration as a means to recruit and to
> regulate the supply of cheap labour. Within the flow of immigration
> to industrialized nations are non-white workers from ex-colonies,
> who are recruited as guest workers, refugees and illegal immigrants,
> in addition to being admitted as regular immigrants. Their tenuous
> status, partly resulting from the political and legal conditions under
> which these immigrants are admitted, makes them exceptionally vul-
> nerable to exploitation. (Bolaria and Li 1988, 36)

One of the problems with this argument is that there is little
evidence that racism is a capitalist conspiracy. It also assumes that

workers and the working-class movement are simply empty vessels that are unthinkingly filled with capitalist-inspired ideology.

Others have addressed these problems by focusing on an alternative side of the capital–labour relationship. Here, the dynamics of class conflict are the key, with the white working class playing a central role in the origins and development of racism (Bonacich 1972; 1976). In capitalist societies, racism and ethnic antagonism emerge from the dynamics between capitalist employers, higher-paid labour, and cheap labour. According to split labour market theory, ethnic and racial conflicts are rooted in differences in the price of labour (Bonacich 1979, 19). Employers hire workers at the cheapest price possible. For historical reasons, workers who move from rural to urban areas or from other countries have often been prepared to offer their labour for less than that of native-born and more established workers. For reasons connected more to accidents of history than to biology, people with darker skin have played the role of cheap labour, while white workers have tended to be higher-paid (Bonacich 1979, 20). The existence of these low-wage workers constitutes a threat to the social and economic position of higher-paid workers; employers will always seek to replace expensive labour with cheap labour. According to this theory, higher-paid workers attempt to reduce competition by imposing restrictions on where and under what conditions lower-priced workers can work. Racial hostility and exclusionary movements arise with the goal of limiting job opportunities for cheaper labour. Racism and ethnic prejudices are the by-products of these competitive labour market dynamics.

Although the split labour market has existed in a variety of forms and places, perhaps the most extreme form was evident in South Africa during the period of apartheid (1948–94). Apartheid was characterized by a strict segregation of races in all spheres of life—education, work, leisure, and place of residence. While the origins of the apartheid system are complex, it came about when white workers sought protection from the competition of lower-priced black workers. White workers convinced the governing authorities and employers that it was in the interests of all white people to maintain a strict separation of races. In the employment sphere, apartheid policies guaranteed more prestigious and better-paid jobs to white people, and also dictated highly discrepant wages between black people and white people. The job reservation system meant that no black person could advance above a white person in the same occupational area, and in some cases black people were completely excluded from certain occupations (Marger 1997, 406). One of the consequences of this policy was the virtual elimination of the class of poor white people from South African society: apartheid was essentially a policy by which black people subsidized white wages and generally affluent lifestyles. Drawing on notions of biological and cultural superiority, many white people believed that because they constituted "the civilized, Christian race," it was their duty "to use their control of the state to prevent racial friction and racial bastardization by ensuring that the races would be separated from one another" (Thompson 1985, quoted in Marger 1997, 409). According to Edna Bonacich, the racial ideologies that accompanied the system of apartheid were essentially justification for the unequal treatment that black Africans experienced at the hands of white South Africans.

Canada has also seen versions of the split labour market (Makabe 1981), though less extreme than in South Africa. Agnes Calliste studied the formation of a split labour market on Canadian railways in the early and mid-twentieth century. She argues that black men were confined to lower-paying jobs such as sleeping car porter, while better-paying jobs such as sleeping car conductor were reserved for white men. According to Calliste, white union members and employers collaborated to keep black men out of better-paying jobs on railways. Black workers were kept in their inferior positions because they were desperately poor and needed the work, and because it was a sign of status among white people to be served by black people (Calliste 1987, 3).

Though more compelling than earlier versions of political economy's analysis of racism, split labour market theory is limited in its scope. While it is useful for understanding and analyzing forms of racism in the past, racially based forms of employment discrimination are now very difficult to create and enforce in countries like Canada, where both domestic and international human rights norms prevent the development of policies or practices that explicitly put one ethnic or racial group at a disadvantage. Indeed, according to Calliste (1987, 11), black workers used the 1953 Fair Employment Practices Act to challenge the discriminatory practices of both railway unions and railway employers.

This model no longer seems suitable for explaining contemporary forms of racism. However, there are softer versions that focus on the broad links between the expression of racism and the everyday

A Political Economy Analysis of Tensions in Alberta

Growing Tension

Whether widespread or isolated, cases of permanent residents being laid off while foreign workers remain exacerbate racial and social tensions which were already beginning to bubble to the surface due to the recession.

Large numbers of recently arrived non-Canadians working and living in Alberta communities have the potential at any time to create discomfort among neighbours as language barriers and cultural differences can challenge and threaten long-time residents and make the newcomers vulnerable and excluded. The rapid influx of foreign workers across the province has strained many communities. Albertans, frankly, have not been as welcoming as they could be. Often bad employers worsen the situation by isolating the workers within the communities.

But when the economy turns south, discomfort can become tension and even full-blown racism. There is legitimate concern that foreign workers may be targeted by frustrated permanent residents scared by the economy.

...

The situation is delicate. Permanent residents have reason to be frustrated at seeing temporary workers employed when the unemployment rate is starting to climb. However, foreign workers came in good faith to work in Canada and to send them home a few months after their arrival also has elements of injustice as well.

...

Both in the interests of minimizing injustice and preventing tension in communities, the AFL [Alberta Federation of Labour] Advocate [for temporary foreign workers] strongly argues that Albertans should remember that the foreign workers did not create the economic downturn and are being negatively effected just as much as permanent residents. Turning frustration, fear and anger toward foreign workers is the wrong target.

Source: Alberta Federation of Labour 2009, 27–28

anxieties and problems of different groups. Economically driven contacts between different groups of people, as well as competition for markets, jobs, housing, and other resources often produce tensions and hostility (Mitchell 2004). Peter Li (1998a) argues that the controversies that occasionally arise in large Canadian cities over the development of "ethnic malls" reflect underlying class dynamics and class-based resentments. The deputy mayor of Markham, Ontario, warned in 1995 that the growing concentration of Chinese people in the city and the growth of malls catering to the Chinese community were causing social tensions; it was also contributing to an exodus of white people from the city. Among other things, the deputy mayor called for restrictions on non-English language signs in the city. According to Li (1998a, 147), the hostility directed toward Chinese businesses had little to do with primordial and supposed natural hostilities between white and Chinese residents. Instead, it was largely connected to Chinese business owners' success in suburban shopping areas, endangering the survival of other small businesses. Part of the hostility reflected fear on the part of white business owners that they might not be able to survive in a competitive and changing marketplace.

In this model, racism is not simply a free-floating attitude that is expressed independent of wider social relations and conflicts. Rather, it constitutes one of the ways that individuals interpret and give meaning to their lives, to their experiences and relationships, and to the tensions and contradictions that they face in the everyday world.

The power-conflict approach allows us to take racism seriously, but without prejudging either the motives behind or the consequences of racism. It also enables us to see the historical and social construction of labels, and to begin to imagine that racism in not an inevitable part of the human condition. If attitudes about the biological and cultural superiority of groups of people are used to make sense of the world, then we need to understand the motives and perspectives of those who articulate those attitudes. We also need to recognize that there is no presumed social consequence associated with such attitudes. "Meanings are in people": racism has a variety of consequences, and these consequences depend on the historical moment; social context; influence of individuals, communities, and organizations; and degree of resistance that groups of racialized people can mount to combat discrimination.

Chapter 3

Immigration Policy

In his April 2008 guest blog on the CBC Manitoba website, Marty Dolin, a former Member of the Legislative Assembly of Manitoba and current Director of the Manitoba Interfaith Immigration Council, noted that public attitudes and public policy have become less "racist and xenophobic," but the culture of the Department of Immigration has not caught up. The Department understands its role to be "gatekeepers," charged with

> protecting "us" against "them"; keeping Canada white and European, protecting our borders against the hoards of Chinese, East Indians, Africans, Roma and Middle Easterners who wish to become part of our great nation.
>
> While I doubt that the individuals who make up the Department of Immigration are, for the most part, overtly and consciously racist and xenophobic, one can only look at the practices and policies of the department and its effects to draw the conclusion that the outcome of these policies and practices are both racist and xenophobic and, of primary importance, detrimental to the economic and social well-being of Canada and a threat to our future as a nation. (CBC Manitoba 2008)

At first blush, the claim that Canada has racist elements to its immigration policies and practices seems absurd. After all, we are one of the most multicultural nations on earth, and we have some of the most open immigration policies of all advanced industrialized nations. Twenty percent of Canadians are born outside of the country, and Canada accepts more immigrants on a per capita basis than almost any other advanced industrialized country in the world. Today, about 80 percent of the approximately quarter-million immigrants we admit per year come from Asia, Africa, the Middle East, the Caribbean, and Latin America; only 20 percent come from Europe and the United States. Sixty years ago, the proportions were reversed, and far more lopsided. In the 1950s nearly 90 percent of all immigrants came from Europe and the United States with the rest of the world supplying a meager 10 percent of immigrants. How could a racist immigration policy result in an outcome where 80 percent of newcomers admitted on a yearly basis are from countries whose majority populations are not defined as "white"? If immigration policy and practice is driven by a continued desire to keep Canada white, then these policies and practices would be abject failures.

There is no question that today's immigration policies are far less discriminatory than they were in the past. However, even if policies are now fairer, they are not necessarily without some racialization of prospective immigrants and immigration streams; they may in addition have some racist overtones (Simmons 1998; 2010).

A Brief History of Racism in Canadian Immigration

There are many historical examples of racial stereotypes playing a role in shaping decisions about who gets into Canada, as well as discriminatory treatment of non-British and non-Protestant European groups following admission to the country. We saw in the Introduction how attitudes that would now be labelled racist were widespread.

While these attitudes did sometimes shift, for the most part British, American, and Western and Northern European immigrants were favoured by officials and the Canadian political elite. While it was felt that white immigrants would assimilate well, at the other end of the spectrum, some groups were seen to be unsuitable for permanent settlement, particularly people from India, the Caribbean, Africa, and various parts of Asia. Though there were some opportunities to come to Canada for members of these groups, usually it was at the request of employers in need of cheap labour. The workers would then often be subject to exclusionary policies, not welcomed as permanent citizens.

Between 1904 and 1908 some five thousand immigrants from India settled in Canada, mainly in British Columbia. Even though they made up a small fraction of the national population, Canadian authorities feared this immigration spiralling out of control. India, like Canada, may have been a part of the British Empire, but South Asians generally were seen as fundamentally different from—and inferior to—the British and Northern and Western Europeans (Bolaria and Li 1988).

There was a curious feature about Canadian immigration policy: Canadian authorities did their best to mask any racist motivations. Officials were at pains to explain that it was not biological race that made East Asians unsuited for life in Canada, but rather their culture. William Lyon Mackenzie King, the Minister of Labour in 1908 and future prime minister of Canada, argued that the need to prevent more Indians from immigrating to Canada was largely for their own good. Given India's "tropical climate," immigrants from that country would possess "manners and customs so unlike our own" that they would not be able to adapt: this would involve "an amount of privation and suffering which renders a discontinuance of such immigration most desirable in the interests of the Indians themselves" (quoted in Bolaria and Li 1988, 191).

Officials also attempted to hide the selective discrimination behind rules and regulations. In 1908 the federal government passed the Continuous Journey Regulation, requiring that immigrants make one continuous sea journey in the course of relocating to Canada. At the time there were no direct steamship connections to Canada from India. An Indian had no choice but to first travel to Hong Kong or to Japan, and then board another steamship to Canada. Continuous journeys were not an option, and so this barred many prospective immigrants from entering Canada.

Canadian officials framed these policies as non-racist so not to undermine British rule in India. In 1897 British Colonial Secretary Joseph Chamberlain claimed that the British Empire "makes no distinction in favour of or against any race or colour" (Bolaria and Li 1988). At the same time, however, British authorities also gave the Dominions of Canada, Australia, and New Zealand the power to determine their own immigration policies. If Canada passed legislation restricting Indian immigration, and based that legislation on overt racism, these restrictions would then undoubtedly create problems for the legitimacy of British rule in India at a time when home rule campaigns were gaining momentum. Indians might naturally conclude, as Mahatma Gandhi did, that they were not part of the same imperial family after all. As a result, Canada developed a means of excluding Indians that seemingly did not involve race. Clearly, the "new racism" that Martin Barker identified in the 1980s was not so new after all.

This restrictive immigration policy was challenged in 1914 when an Indian businessman encouraged a group of would-be immigrants. Gurdit Singh persuaded 376 individuals, many of whom were dependants of immigrants who had settled in Canada before the regulation took effect, to pay for passage to Canada on a vessel called the *Komagata Maru*. The ship travelled from India to Canada, with stops in Shanghai; Hong Kong; and Moji, Japan, along the way (Johnson 1989, 28–34). Because of those stops, the ship was in violation of the continuous journey stipulation. The *Komagata Maru* arrived in Vancouver harbour in May 1914, but passengers were not allowed to disembark. The ship and its passengers were forced to wait in Vancouver harbour for two months while negotiations between immigration officials and the Indian businessman took place. The Canadian government did allow a small number of passengers to disembark, but eventually the ship was forced out of Vancouver harbour at gunpoint (Johnson 1989).

African American immigration

Canadian policies regarding the admission of black immigrants were contradictory. Before the American Civil War, Canada was the end point of the Underground Railroad, a route that enabled escaped slaves to seek freedom. An estimated thirty thousand ex-slaves settled in Canada, mainly in Southern Ontario. Earlier, both free and enslaved black people were admitted when they came north following the American War of Independence. As part of the larger Loyalist migration to Canada from the United States, many came to Canada with the explicit permission of British colonial authorities and many settled in Nova Scotia. Slaves remained slaves under the ownership of the white Loyalists, but free black people who came north were promised both their continued freedom and land to settle. What many of the free black people found instead was continued prejudice and segregation, not to mention foot-dragging when it came to the distribution of the land that they had been promised. Those who were given land often received plots that were of poor quality, whereas white Loyalists received more, and better, land.

In the late nineteenth and early twentieth centuries, African Americans living on the American plains became interested in the prospect of homesteading on the Canadian prairies. Some African Americans trickled over the border and settled in communities in Alberta and Saskatchewan before World War I. Even though Canada was eager to recruit American and Northern European immigrants to populate the prairies, not all Americans were wanted or preferred. Many Canadians feared black immigration from the US on the grounds that black and white people "could never get along," and because the former "caused problems" wherever they settled. Drawing on the perceived race relations in the US, the Edmonton Board of Trade launched a petition to put an end to black immigration in 1910:

> We cannot admit as any factor the argument that these people may be good farmers or good citizens. It is a matter of common knowledge that it has been proved in the United States that negroes and whites cannot live in proximity without the occurrence of revolting lawlessness, and the development of bitter race hatred. .... We are anxious that such a problem should not be introduced in this fair land at present enjoying a reputation for freedom from such lawlessness as has developed in all sections of the United States where there is no considerable negro element. There is no reason to believe that we have here a higher order of civilization, or that the introduction of a negro problem here would have different results. (Quoted in Shepard 1991, 25–26)

The federal government, concerned with the "Negro problem" eventually took measures to prevent African Americans from moving to Canada. In 1911 the federal government passed an order-in-council prohibiting "immigrants belonging to the Negro race, which race is deemed unsuitable to the climate and requirements of Canada." The federal government also sent immigration agents to Oklahoma to specifically discourage African Americans from considering moving north to Canada (Shepard 1991).

Chinese immigration

Chinese immigrants first started trickling into Canada from the United States in the late 1850s as part of the Fraser Valley gold rush. During the early 1880s, Chinese workers were seen to be essential for the construction of the transcontinental railroad. Several thousand were actively recruited. After the railroad was completed in 1885, the Canadian government instituted a $50 tax on all Chinese immigrants to Canada, hoping to deter further arrivals. But more continued to arrive. In 1899 the tax was increased to $100, and in 1903 to $500. It is estimated that between 1899 and 1923, this tax raised over three million dollars. Chinese immigrants were the only group required to pay the tax. By 1923 the federal government imposed a near-complete ban on Chinese immigration through the Chinese Immigration Act. It is estimated that eighty thousand Chinese immigrants came to Canada between 1878 and 1923; between 1923 and 1947, a total of seven Chinese immigrants were allowed into Canada (Li 1998a).

Some historians say that at this time European Canadians had a deep psychological antipathy to East Asians. Peter Ward (2002, 12) argues that "white British Columbians yearned for a racially homogenous society." The "psychological tensions derived from white society's desire for racial homogeneity, a drive continually stimulated by the racially plural condition" of the province, led members of white society to push for anti-Chinese immigration legislation.

The economic interests of different groups of European Canadians shaped their attitudes. Employers held generally favourable views and opinions about East Asians. Andrew Onderdonk the contractor for the westernmost sections of the transcontinental railroad, was convinced that the railroad could not be completed without Chinese labour (Satzewich 1989). Onderdonk understood Chinese immigrants to be industrious and hard working. Since they did not have families in Canada or any political clout, they were also anonymous and disposable in a way that European Canadian workers were not, which partly explains why they were given the most dangerous jobs on the railway construction crews. Canada maintained an open door to Chinese migration until the railroad was completed in 1885. By then, however, employers in mining, canning, lumber, and manufacturing had started to employ Chinese workers. There was a clamour from employers for continued Chinese migration.

Chinese workers could also be hired for about half of the wages as European Canadian workers, which was another significant incentive. No surprise then that agitation against Chinese immigrants came mainly from ranks of European Canadian workers. White workers in British Columbia organized themselves into groups such as the Anti-Chinese Association, the Anti-Chinese Union, the Anti-Mongolian Association, the Asiatic Exclusion League, and the

Workingmen's Protective Association, among others (Roy 1989). Existing unions like the Knights of Labour also opposed Chinese immigration (Goutor 2007).

Many small business owners in Vancouver, Victoria, and other cities in western Canada also opposed Chinese immigration, in part because as Chinese people started their own businesses they increased competition in restaurant, laundry, and domestic service sectors. In addition to restrictive immigration legislation, other legislation was passed in order to prevent Chinese businesspeople from successfully competing with white people. The goal was to keep Chinese people in a position where they had no choice but to earn a wage, and preferably a low one, in order to survive.

Between the desired Northern European immigrants and the less suitable darker-skinned immigrants were "the non-preferred." These were the "in-between" peoples from Southern and Eastern Europe (Satzewich 2000). Canadian authorities were ambivalent about these groups, in part because of uncertainties about where they fit in prevailing racial hierarchies and ideologies. Even though they were, geographically speaking, European, they seemed different from the more familiar Northern and Western Europeans. Supporters of these immigrants, like Clifford Sifton, the Minister of the Interior in the Laurier government at the end of the nineteenth century, famously described Ukrainians as "stalwart peasants in the sheepskin coats"; they were valuable additions to Canadian society if only because "born on the soil, whose forefathers had been farmers for generations, with a stout wife and half-a-dozen children … [they are of] good quality" (quoted in Lehr 1991, 38). He was optimistic that with time and following opportunity to rub shoulders with better classes of British and Northern European immigrants on the prairies they could be transformed into good Canadians. Others resisted settlement from Southern and Eastern Europe: these people were swarthy, smelled of garlic, were crude, drank too much, and were destined to bring the country down. Sifton's critics called them "Sifton's pets." Others called them "the Scum of Europe." In 1930 Stephen Leacock, one of Canada's most celebrated humourists, wrote that the north-west provinces, especially, were "badly damaged" as a result of the great foreign immigration before World War I.

From the point of view of the Russians and Galicians [Ukrainians], etc., this meant improvement for the north-west. Not so from ours.

Learning English and living under the British flag may make a British subject in the legal sense, but not in the real sense, in the light of national history and continuity. ... A little dose of them may even by variation, do good, like a minute dose of poison in a medicine. ... I am not saying that we should absolutely shut out and debar the European foreigner, as we should and do shut out the Oriental. But we should in no way facilitate his coming. Not for him the free ocean transit, not the free coffee of the immigrant shed, nor the free land, not the found job, nor the guaranteed anything. He is lucky if he is let in "on his own." (Quoted in Porter 1965, 67)

Leacock was not alone. Non-preferred immigrants tended to be admitted on a "hold your nose" basis; better than nobody at all, but certainly not ideal.

Post–World War II

The end of World War II marked a major turning point in the history of Canadian immigration policy. The Chinese Immigrant Act was repealed, as were some of the more noxious restrictions over Chinese Canadian civil and political rights. Chinese Canadians could vote in elections after 1947, and they could become lawyers and pharmacists, positions that had been denied them because they were not allowed on voters' lists prior to 1947. Also in 1947, the federal government rescinded the Continuous Journey Regulation and allowed Indians in Canada the right to vote in federal elections. By 1952, the federal government opened the door—ever so slightly—to immigration from India, Pakistan, and Ceylon (now Sri Lanka) by establishing yearly quotas of 150, 100, and 50 immigrants per year from these countries, respectively (Bolaria and Li 1988, 173). Jews—who before and during the war had come to Canada to escape Nazi Germany but had been turned back through sheer anti-Semitism—began to gain entry to the country after the war (Abella and Troper 1982).

The post–World War II international political environment played a role in tempering officially sanctioned discrimination within the immigration system. As we saw above, the world had become much more aware of the atrocities committed against Jews and others in the name of race and racial purity. Government policies that were grounded on explicitly racist assumptions about the inferiority of groups of people were discredited both politically and scientifically.

Though the wider political climate around the world was changing, these changes did not lead Canadians to completely abandon race and ethnicity as criteria to assess immigrants (Iacovetta 2006). Canada began to develop a different means for exclusion. As Prime Minister Mackenzie King explained in a now well-known speech in the House of Commons in 1950,

> The policy of the government is to foster the growth of the population of Canada by encouraging immigration. The government will seek by legislation, regulation and vigorous administration, to ensure the careful selection and permanent settlement of such numbers of immigrants as can advantageously be absorbed into our national economy. ... With regard to the selection of immigrants much has been said about discrimination. I wish to make it quite clear that Canada is perfectly within her rights in selecting persons whom we regard as desirable future citizens. It is not a "fundamental human right" of any alien to enter Canada. It is a privilege. It is a matter of domestic policy.
> . . . There will, I am sure, be general agreement with the view that the people of Canada do not wish, as a result of mass immigration, to make a fundamental alteration in the character of our population.
> (Canada 1947, 2644–47)

King made it clear that while Canada was willing to open the door to immigration slightly, it could and should continue to discriminate in its immigration policy. Further, King's unwillingness to alter "the character of our population" signalled a desire to keep Canada predominantly white (Li 2003). Though race was not listed as a category, the 1952 Immigration Act gave the Department of Citizenship and Immigration considerable leeway in the criteria available to prohibit entry to the country (Satzewich 1991).

Race may have been absent in policy, but it was present in the interpretation and administration of that policy. During the 1950s and early 1960s, there was a widespread conviction within immigration circles, and among the Canadian public, that black people were racially inferior, caused problems where they settled, and were unable to adjust to social and climate conditions. One immigration official explained in a memo to his colleagues in 1958,

> It is not by accident that coloured British Subjects other than negligible numbers from the United Kingdom are excluded from Canada. ... They do not assimilate readily and pretty much vegetate to a low standard of

living. Despite what has been said to the contrary, many cannot adapt themselves to our climatic conditions. (Director of Immigration 1955)

Officials were equally wary of admitting immigrants from India and other parts of Asia.

The attitude toward non-white immigration within the immigration department started to change in the early 1960s. Racially based selection criteria were formally abandoned in 1962 in part because the racist nature of Canadian immigration policy was an international embarrassment for Canada. Lester Pearson's 1957 Nobel Peace Prize for his contributions to the settlement of the Suez crisis boosted Canada's image as an international peacekeeper. This image was, however, undermined by the racism of its immigration policy, drawing criticism by some leaders of newly independent Caribbean states.

Contemporary Immigration Policy

There is little if any officially sanctioned racism within Canadian immigration policy today. Canada has a universally applicable points system for the selection of skilled workers and professionals, based on education, experience, language abilities, and skills. In addition, a job offer from a Canadian employer translates into points. The immigration system prioritizes family reunification and humanitarian obligations to refugees. Preferences based overtly on ethnicity no longer exist in Canada's current legislation, which is a far cry from the 1952 Immigration Act.

Despite significant changes in legislation, and the increasing range of sending countries over the past 50 years, it is worth a close look at how the Department of Citizenship and Immigration admits, screens, and deports immigrants and refugees. Critics have argued that even though race was abandoned as a selection criterion in the early 1960s, at least four areas remain where some racism is alleged to continue to operate.

First, critics claim that the locations of Canadian immigration offices abroad continue to reflect an informal preference for white immigrants. In 2008 there were 43 immigration offices abroad: 12 were in the US, Australia, and Europe with the remainder in South and Central America, Africa, the Middle East, and Asia. Thus, even though immigrants from the US, Europe, and Australia constitute only about 20 percent of total flow to Canada, 27 percent of immigration visa processing offices are located in these countries. This disproportion in resources leads to differences in processing times. The fact that approval for certain categories of immigration can take over six years for candidates from Africa, the Middle East, or Asia, and between only 2.5 and 3.5 years for candidates from the United States or Europe, suggests that there is still an informal preference system at work.

Second, immigration officers' discretionary authority may put applications by peoples of colour at a disadvantage. Before the introduction of the 2002 Immigration and Refugee Protection Act, the selection factors within the points system included a category called "personal suitability." Up to 10 points could be awarded to applicants based on the immigration officer's judgment. Critics argued that personal suitability points were more often awarded to white applicants. Sociologists Alan Anderson and James Frideres (1980, 227; see also Jakubowski 1997, 21) explain that in the early 1980s "depending on the selection officer's bias [or views about racial groups], the applicant can receive zero points in this category, thus lessening the applicant's chance of entering Canada."

The selection system no longer gives specific points for personal suitability. However, immigration officers still have the authority to make "substituted evaluations": they may admit an applicant who has not otherwise earned a "pass mark" in the points system. This is called positive discretion. Conversely, they can deny entry to an applicant who has earned enough points on the existing selection factors using negative discretion. The Canadian Race Relations Foundation (2001) and social scientists Evelyn Kallen (2003, 112) and Frances Henry and Carol Tator (2010) all argue that an immigration officer's ability to make a substituted evaluation is one way that racial bias continues to creep into the system (Bouchard and Carroll 2002). Positive discretion is more likely to be given to white applicants; negative discretion is more commonly exercised against applicants from people of colour.

The third area where the Canadian system has been criticized is the refugee determination system. The Safe Third Country Agreement with the United States, which took effect in 2004, is part of an effort to reduce the number of refugee claims that are made on Canadian soil. The Canadian Council on Refugees explains,

Under the Safe Third Country Agreement, the US and Canada each declared the other country safe for refugees and established the general principle that refugee claimants should make their claim in the first of these countries that they reach. Thus refugees who are in the US are expected to pursue their claim in the US, rather than seeking protection in Canada. Similarly, those in Canada are expected to apply in Canada. However, in practice few asylum seekers move from Canada to the US to make a refugee claim: the Agreement is about preventing people who are in the US, or traveling through the US, from making a refugee claim in Canada. (Canadian Council for Refugees 2010)

Marty Dolin (see p. 31) argues that the Agreement is "consistent" with the Department of Immigration's original intent to keep "refugees, mainly people of colour, from entering Canada to seek protection. It protects the white European vision of Canada by further closing the gates and, as a bonus, it transfers the work of screening refugee claims to the Americans" (CBC Manitoba 2008).

The stated purpose of the agreement is to deter "asylum shopping"—situations where individuals seek refugee status in one country even though they may have already secured a safe haven elsewhere. However, critics argue that Canada is turning its back on genuine refugees, indirectly returning them to potentially dangerous, strife-torn situations.

The agreement has been subject to legal challenges brought forward by organizations like Amnesty International, the Canadian Council of Churches, and the Canadian Council of Refugees. These organizations argue that the agreement violates Canada's international human rights obligations and the Canadian Charter of Rights and Freedoms. The Federal Court of Appeal disagrees, and has allowed the Agreement to remain in place.

Finally, detention and deportation policies have also opened Canada to criticism (Pratt 2005). The 2002 Immigration and Refugee Protection Act allows immigration authorities to detain permanent residents and foreign nationals arriving in Canada if there is a genuine fear under one of the following conditions: a potential flight risk, a potential risk to the public, or a concern about false identity. Individuals who are suspected of not being genuine visitors to Canada, who are found working in Canada illegally, who have overstayed their visa, who have had their refugee claims rejected, or who claim asylum in Canada are the main categories of people detained by the Canadian Border Services Agency (CBSA). There are three immigration detention centers in Canada: in Toronto, Montreal, and Vancouver. Individuals can also be detained at provincial correctional facilities if they are apprehended far from these three facilities.

In a recent study of detention and deportation, sociologist Anna Pratt found that "the vast majority of those detained at ... [the Toronto detention centre] are nonwhite, male and between the ages of twenty and forty." In her snapshot of the detainee population at the Toronto Centre in February 2000, she found a total of 85 detainees, 32 of whom were from Asia, 19 from Central and South America, 14 from Africa, 9 from the West Indies, 8 from Eastern Europe, one from Western Europe, and one from the Middle East (Pratt 2005, 45–46). Pratt argues that the definition of "risk" as interpreted by border officials continues to be subject to ethnic and racial stereotyping. Though not "readily apparent from the official view of law or policy," she argues that "the spectre of the 'dark' alien so familiar in Canadian immigration history" continues to impact the treatment of immigrants and refugees (Pratt 2005, 138).

It is difficult to assess whether racism informs some, all, or none of these policies and practices. As we noted in Chapter 1, racism is difficult to measure empirically. Oftentimes it has to be inferred either through the examination of consequences, or the examination of the code language that makes oblique reference to race. Assessing admission procedures is often complex. There is, for example, no systematic evidence to suggest that before the 2002 changes to the selection system, peoples of colour were given fewer points for personal suitability. Nor is there any solid empirical evidence to suggest that darker-skinned immigrants are systematically more likely to suffer from negative discretion and white applicants are more likely to enjoy positive discretion. In fact, negative discretion seems to be exercised rarely.

Though the location of immigration offices and differences in processing times may seem to imply discrimination, the situation is not unambiguous. Officials argue that disparities in processing times reflect difficulties with communication, transportation, and information gathering systems in different parts of the world. Processing times also depend on the completeness of the applications and concerns about fraud. Moreover, security and health checks are more complicated and involved in regions like

Africa and the Middle East than they are in Vienna or London. Another issue is that Canadian immigration offices in the US process a considerable volume of applicants for permanent residence in Canada from individuals already living in Canada as temporary residents. Only a small proportion of their workload consists of applications from native-born Americans living in the United States. In other words, our immigration offices in the US do not seem to be fast-tracking Americans simply because they are presumed to be white.

Domestic Servants and Migrant Workers

There are two other areas of immigration where racist overtones may be present: the migration to Canada of domestic workers and the migration of seasonal agricultural workers from Mexico and the Caribbean.

Domestics

Many native-born Canadians avoid domestic and child care–related work because of the low pay. Child care, in fact, is one of the most poorly paid occupations in the country. In 2005 the median earnings of child care workers in Canada were $21,980. The median earnings of all occupations in the country were $41,401.

Many middle-class families require two or more earners to make ends meet and to maintain their standard of living. As a result, some families must hire a domestic worker to look after their children (or elderly parents), to cook, and to clean their homes. Like other employers in low-wage sectors of the economy, middle-class households face perennial labour recruitment and retention problems. Does racialization and racism play a role in this labour supply?

In the late 1940s and early 1950s, women from Europe were recruited to come to Canada to fill these jobs. Canadian authorities thought that British and European women would be valuable additions to both our labour force and our society. In the short term, they helped solve labour shortages. In the long term, the expectation and hope was that they would marry, have children, and contribute to what Mackenzie King called "the character of our population" (Danys 1986). Once here, however, they found the work difficult and poorly paid compared to other jobs; they soon found better-paying work elsewhere. Others got married, had children of their own, and withdrew from the labour force—some temporarily and some permanently. The various immigration schemes that brought British and European women to Canada as domestic servants following World War II did not offer a permanent solution to this labour problem.

In the late 1950s and early 1960s, Canadians started to look to other parts of the world for women to undertake this domestic work. The English-speaking Caribbean was close by, and many men and women from the islands were eager to leave. Even though there were barriers preventing Caribbean immigration, there were exceptions in the policy. In the 1950s, nurses and stenographers were allowed into Canada on a limited basis; immigration officials defined them as cases of "exceptional merit" (Stasiulis and Bakan 2005, 107). The other exception was for domestic workers. Canada instituted a quota system for female domestic workers in the mid 1950s, recruiting Caribbean women—seen as good sources of domestic labour—in the 1950s and 1960s. They were stereotyped as nurturing, good natured, and passive; and they could speak English. They also had few economic opportunities in their countries of origin, so would accept low wages. But there were concerns on the part of immigration officials. Like European women who came before them, after a few years in Canada, many found better-paying, more agreeable work in other sectors of the economy. Furthermore, while they might be good workers, they also had relatives in the Caribbean who might one day want to join them in Canada. And some day they might marry Canadian men and have children of their own. Would this lead to race problems? The Deputy Minister of Citizenship and Immigration suggested in 1964,

> One single female domestic servant may take a year or two to become established but she may then begin to sponsor brothers, sisters, fiancé, parents, at a fairly rapid rate. The one unsponsored worker may meet someone's need for a domestic servant for a year or two, but the result may be ten or twenty sponsored immigrants of dubious value to Canada and who may well cause insoluble social problems. ... I am greatly concerned that we may be facing a West Indian sponsorship explosion. (Deputy Minister of Citizenship and Immigration 1964)

The quota arrangements for domestic servant migration from the Caribbean remained in place until 1973 when immigration authorities developed a policy, the Foreign Domestic Movement (FDM), designed to draw women from the Caribbean into Canada on a temporary basis (Arat-Koc 1992, 230). Instead of admitting female domestics as permanent residents, the FDM gave them temporary work permits with supposedly fixed end dates. The rules also made it hard to change employers. The women who came would work for low wages but have little option of becoming permanent residents. Sociologist Sedef Arat-Koc (1992, 231) argues that "the temporary work permit system worked like a 'revolving door,' expecting those who had worked in Canada for a few years to leave while new workers replaced them."

In the 1960s and early 1970s, many Western European countries also used various kinds of temporary worker schemes to solve labour shortages; what they found was that these schemes tended to break down, particularly if the jobs were permanent (Castles and Miller 2003). This is what happened in Canada with the FDM. Many of the women who were given temporary one- or two-year labour contracts renewed these contracts for consecutive years. Though they were technically only temporary workers, many became permanent members of the labour force, as well as members of society. But they were caught in a legal limbo with fewer rights than Canadian citizens or permanent residents. Some women started to form relationships and have families. Their precarious political and legal position subjected them to exploitation by their employers, given the threat of a discontinued contract. Since they could not vote in elections, they were poorly advocated for by politicians.

In this context, organizations like the International Coalition to End Domestic Exploitation (INTERCEDE) were formed, and the immigration department eventually modified program rules to allow women to apply for permanent residence after a two-year probationary period. In this new Live-in Caregiver Program (LCP), first developed in 1992, domestic workers were required to remain under the same employment contract and could not change employers without the permission of their original employer (in addition, an immigration officer had to be convinced of the legitimacy of the reason for the change). They were also required to live in the home of their employer. In order to qualify for permanent residence, they had to demonstrate their "social adaptation" to Canadian society through volunteer work or community involvement; they also had to prove a degree of "financial security" (Arat-Koc 1992, 234).

As their rights improved under the LCP movement, so too did their resistance to the conditions under which they were employed. Over time, Caribbean women came to be defined by employment agencies, recruiters, and some employers as troublesome workers. Some were unwilling to do all the work that was asked of them, like staying late on short notice to babysit (Stasiulis and Bakan 2005, 78). Employers were becoming less enamoured with the Caribbean as a source of domestic labour. One domestic placement agency owner in the 1990s noted that it was harder to find employment for a West Indian than it was for a Filipino. While claiming to tell prospective clients to let the agency find the best candidate for the job, the owner nevertheless noted that "we have a hard time placing West Indians in jobs. I know that this is discrimination, but they are looking for people to do jobs and to live as tenants. Sometimes the husband is really racist. Or the employers will say that their children are afraid of someone who is of a different colour" (Stasiulis and Bakan 2005, 78–79).

Employers express preferences, and certain ethnic stereotypes— sometimes stated, sometimes unstated—play a role in in shaping those preferences. A domestic placement agency owner gave an example to researchers Daiva Stasiulis and Abigail Bakan:

> I have a client, a man, who said that he couldn't stand the hairdo of a girl I sent to him for an interview. ... He had nothing against Blacks, but it was all in little braids, and he hates that. His wife wanted to hire her. He and his wife had a terrible fight over it. ... The couple called me up because they were arguing. I said, "I know you want her, but I won't recommend her. Because it's not fair to you, and it's not fair to the girl." (Stasiulis and Bakan 2005, 72)

Filipina domestic workers began to trickle into Canada in the 1980s under the FDM. By 1995 the Philippines became the top source country for domestic servants; today, nearly 90 percent of domestic workers coming to Canada under the LCP are from that country alone (Trumper and Wong 2007, 163). The perception that Filipinas were more docile, less liable to complain or raise trouble, and were hard-working influenced this change. But one domestic placement agency owner argues that Filipina domestic workers are not the perfect solution to child care, given that some employers see them as too passive when it comes to raising and disciplining children. However, it is this "passivity" that makes them easier to deal with as employees.

> Most of my placements are from the Philippines, more than 50 percent, by far the highest percentage. Filipino nannies are very soft, they don't stimulate the children. They cannot control the children, it doesn't come naturally to them. Socially, the Filipino nanny comes from a culture where they are extremely respectful of elders, of authority, and they are trained not to offer their views too aggressively. ... Filipino nannies were always more giving, very professional in a sense. But now the shine is coming off the Filipino nanny. ... I know this, because some clients have told me this. It doesn't apply to all the Filipinos. Generally, Filipinos are good with housework, but not always. You could always get a dud. (Stasiulis and Bakan 2005, 79–80)

As the employment agency owner quoted above suggests, it may be that the perception of "docility" is not as simple and straightforward as all would like. There is a mix of positive and negative attitudes toward Filipinos. While it would be tempting to say that this was only racialization, it does suggest that at least some Canadians think of Filipina difference in biological and deterministic terms. As we saw above, Canadian society still apparently believes certain groups of people are suitable for some kinds of work but not others.

Migrant farm workers

Leamington, Ontario, prides itself on being the tomato capital of Canada. In fact, Leamington has more greenhouse acreage under cultivation than the entire US greenhouse industry combined (Windsor-Essex Economic Development Corporation 2010).

Another interesting fact about Leamington is that in a town of only thirty-one thousand residents, the grocery store shelves are stocked with imported products from Mexico, and Mexican restaurants abound. Mexican workers come to Leamington every year as part of a larger yearly migration that enables over twenty thousand workers from Mexico and various Caribbean countries to work in agricultural operations in Canada. They come under special Caribbean and Mexican Seasonal Agricultural Workers

Programs, under the following conditions: they work for a specific named employer; they cannot quit or change jobs without the permission of their employer and the agency that administers the program. They may work in Canada for up to eight months per year and are provided with housing (part of the costs of which are deducted from their pay), and employers cover half of their transportation cost to Canada. They pay into the Canada Pension and Employment Insurance plans. They work in greenhouses and in apple, peach, and cherry orchards. They pick everything from strawberries, cucumbers, tomatoes, cabbages, and cauliflower to tobacco. They also prune pine trees in the summer so that the Christmas trees we buy in December have a conical shape. Workers from the Caribbean first started coming to Canada in 1966, in what immigration officials described as a small experimental program to address a temporary shortage of workers in Ontario agriculture (Satzewich 1991). Now, workers from the Caribbean and Mexico are a significant part of the agricultural labour force in almost every Canadian province.

A recent World Bank (2006) report describes the Caribbean and Mexican Seasonal Agricultural Workers Program as a "win-win" scheme. Workers from the Caribbean and Mexico benefit because it provides them with earnings that are better than what they might expect in their home countries. Mexico and Caribbean countries benefit because it provides them with foreign currency. Canadian society benefits because a healthy agricultural industry helps expand higher skilled jobs in areas like transportation, construction, and processing. And of course, farmers benefit because it provides them with a reliable labour force. Canadian consumers can rely less on imports. Indeed, the World Bank (as well as the governments of both Canada and Mexico) argue that this is a best-practice program that should be expanded to other sectors of the economy and to other parts of the world.

This arrangement sounds good in theory. But as with domestic worker migration, there are racialized overtones at play. Is it an accident that the workers are mainly black and Mexican? Why do we rarely see white people working in the fields? In many respects, the story behind the Caribbean and Mexican Seasonal Agricultural Workers Programs is similar to the story behind domestic service. It begins with a perennial labour recruitment and retention problem and ends with Canadian immigration authorities finding racialized workers from other parts of the world who are seen as good enough to work in Canada but not good enough to stay.

The history of paid farm labour follows similar patterns to domestic work. In the late 1940s and early 1950s, Eastern European refugees and Polish war veterans, among others, were seen as the ideal source of farm labour. In 1950 one Southern Ontario newspaper boldly claimed, "Without immigrants you don't grow cash crops!" (quoted in Satzewich 1991). Immigrants, the newspaper explained, were needed because they worked harder than Canadians. They were willing to do the jobs that Canadians turned down. Sometimes after working on the farms for a few years, they bought farms of their own, just like the homesteaders did on the prairies 50 years earlier. And, of course, from a wider perspective, the immigrants were white, which would contribute to Mackenzie King's desire to maintain the "character of the population."

Some postwar Eastern and Western European immigrants did eventually buy their own farms. In fact, some became spectacularly successful at farming. Some Dutch farm families whose land was deliberately flooded by the retreating German army as World War II was winding down were aggressively recruited by immigration authorities to come to Canada in the late 1940s and early 1950s. They eventually became involved in greenhouse production (Satzewich 1991). Their children and grandchildren are now the owners of some of the gigantic greenhouses in Leamington and other places that employ workers from the Caribbean and Mexico.

In other cases, though, the Europeans who were admitted did not stay working on farms for long. Many left agricultural employment shortly after their contracts expired and found better-paying work elsewhere (Satzewich 1991).

As the Displaced Person refugee camps emptied out by the early 1950s, the supply of Eastern European immigrants decreased. Western European economic prosperity in the mid 1950s meant that it was harder for immigration officials to find "desirable" European immigrants. But farmers still needed workers, and so they began to think beyond Britain and Northern Europe. Ontario farmers wanted the federal government to allow them to hire workers from the Caribbean to help with the harvest. The problem, of course, was racial stereotypes and prejudices. Canada was uneasy about admitting black people; there was already anxiety about domestic workers and the cases of "exceptional merit." Black men were seen as the source of a potentially bigger race problem than black women.

Following the atrocities of World War II, Canadian immigration authorities were reluctant to overtly reject Caribbean workers. Caribbean governments and Ontario farmers lobbied to allow workers from the Caribbean to come to Canada, but government immigration officials only changed their position in the mid-1960s. The Caribbean Seasonal Workers Program was created in 1966, the basic structure of which is still with us today. In 1974 Mexico was added to this program to create the Mexican Seasonal Agricultural Workers Program.

One of the interesting features of these two temporary worker programs is that they have generally not turned into movements of permanent settlers. Workers coming to Canada under these arrangements are not allowed to permanently settle. Nor are there any special provisions to reward workers who have returned year after year; their applications for permanent residence are not treated any differently than that of an applicant who has never set foot in the country (Preibisch 2004).

It seems that some people are good enough to work in Canada but not good enough to stay. This, again, is where racialization and, even more, racism come into play. There are two dimensions to the Seasonal Agricultural Workers Programs worth noting. First, until 1966, federal immigration authorities denied opportunities for workers from the Caribbean to come to Canada on racist grounds. When workers were eventually allowed to participate in the agricultural industry, immigration authorities designed a program that prevented these workers from permanently settling in Canada. Workers were admitted on a seasonal contractual basis and were required to leave Canada every year, regardless of any wishes to remain. While this solved farmers' labour recruitment and retention problems, the perception remains that that Caribbeans would cause the emergence of race problems if too many were allowed to settle here permanently. They might start families and sponsor relatives, potentially resulting in the growth of the black population of Canada; in the mid-1960s, immigration officials were anxious about this possible outcome (Satzewich 1991).

Second, when the program was first created, workers were confined to a narrow range of field-work operations on farms. They were not allowed into other areas of the economy. In fact, employers in the fruit and vegetable processing industry wanted to employ them as factory workers under broadly similar terms. But immigration officials refused: Caribbean men were "adapted" to field work, but allowing them to work inside rural factories would surely cause problems. One immigration official explained:

> [Processing] operations require a high content of female labour and to introduce Jamaican males into the plants and provide accommodation adjacent to that used by domestic female labour could create social difficulties. Moreover, the Jamaican male is adapted to field rather than factory work and while the processors felt that they could train them to do the latter, it does not seem they could hope to staff plants entirely with this labour. These factors are not present in field employment. The Jamaicans are adapted to the work, the work units are smaller and there need not be a male-female, or even a Jamaican-domestic mix of male labour on any one operation. (Manpower Services 1966)

Black men might safely be allowed to work in the fields, under carefully controlled circumstances. But in factories, it was considered dangerous for them to work alongside white women, and the request was denied.

Even though these migration streams may no longer be sustained by racist ideas, their origins in part from racist attitudes suggest that the legacy may well be biased treatment of Caribbean and Mexican agricultural workers today.

Proving conclusively that there are elements of racism in current immigration policies and procedures is difficult. Decisions about who gets into Canada are the result of a complex process in which a variety of considerations come into play, not least of which are procedural fairness, security, and the economic well-being of immigrants, and of Canadian society more generally. While it seems unlikely that the system is rife with institutional racism, processes of racialization no doubt play some role in shaping who gets into Canada.

Chapter 4

Racism and Aboriginal Peoples

Canada's relationship with Aboriginal peoples is complex. Public opinion polls show that Canadians have generally high levels of sympathy (Ponting and Kiely 1997); however, this sympathy evaporates quickly at times of protest, when Native peoples block roads or occupy a public space to draw attention to their conditions. Polls further indicate that Canadians generally know little about Aboriginal issues and do not see them as a high federal priority (Ponting and Kiely 1997). The 2010 Vancouver Olympics placed Native cultural symbols prominently in the opening and closing ceremonies. But in spite of this public usage, many Canadians show little concern for the poverty and high levels of unemployment faced by Aboriginal peoples. Few people of Aboriginal descent could afford the price of an Olympic ticket.

This chapter begins with the issue of identity. There are a number of terms used to describe Aboriginal peoples, including First Nations, First Peoples, Native peoples, Metis, Inuit, Status Indian, and Non-Status Indian. Interesting questions arises here: Is defining individuals by their group membership a form of racism? Is providing group-based benefits to a given ethnic group another? After considering this issue, this chapter recounts some of the history of racism experienced by Native peoples. The chapter concludes with a look at the current conditions of Aboriginal peoples.

Identity and Band Membership

Former University of Colorado Ethnic Studies Professor Ward Churchill identifies as a Native American but was recently discovered to not have "objective" Native American ancestry. He was criticized by some for being a fraud, and the discovery undermined his authority to speak about Native American issues (Brown 2007). Churchill's case is not all that different from that of Archibald Belaney, the English immigrant who constructed an Ojibwa identity for himself as "Grey Owl." Grey Owl lived in Northern Saskatchewan in the 1920s and 1930s, wrote numerous articles and books about "his people" and conservation issues. During one of his speaking tours to England in the 1930s, doubts about his true identity began to surface. Following his death in 1938 it became clear that he was not really who he was portraying himself to be. When the news of his English background emerged, his publisher ceased printing his books; some books were even withdrawn from sale. It has been argued that the conservation causes that Grey Owl promoted during his lifetime were badly damaged by the unmasking of his identity.

Referring to the Churchill case in the United States, Roland Chrisjohn, Professor of Native Studies at St. Thomas University in New Brunswick, explained that the "determination of rights based on race is dangerous and wrong. Being an Indian is not and has never been a racial matter, and merely having sex does not create the next generation of Indians—spirituality, history and language are more important than genes" (Cormier 2007).

Though they occurred decades apart and in two different countries, the cases of Churchill and Belaney raise sticky questions about identity. What role does objective ancestry play in determining group membership? Other issues are genetic heritage, identifying with a group, and the right to use this identification to be an advocate.

In circumstances where societies do not attach special privileges, or special limitations, to individuals because of their membership in a particular group, these kinds of questions might be interesting, but in the wider scheme of things they don't really matter that much. For example, if someone in Canada today without any Latvian ancestors claims to be Latvian, learns the Latvian language, observes Latvian cultural and religious practices, and writes and speaks passionately about Latvia and/or Latvian Canadian issues, we might think the person a curiosity. Since individuals with Latvian ancestry or of Latvian identity do not face special restrictions, or have special rights or privileges, someone claiming to be Latvian is largely inconsequential. If, however, the government of Canada decided that Latvians should have special rights—say to cut down a certain number of trees from city boulevards each year in order to use in a Latvian religious ritual—then the question of who is Latvian, and how "Latvianness" is defined, becomes more consequential. After all, we would not want people passing as Latvian in order to cut down city trees to simply feed their wood stoves.

Though this may seem to be a rather far-fetched example, this is part of the reason why the definition of Aboriginal peoples is so important in Canada today. To be sure, the issue of whether we call someone Aboriginal, First Nation, Metis, Status Indian, Non-Status Indian, or Inuit matters to people for personal reasons. But the issue of who belongs to their group, and how group membership is defined, also matters for political and economic reasons. There are social, political and economic consequences to these definitions because for Aboriginal people, there are special rights, and special limitations, attached to these identities.

The Constitution of Canada recognizes the "existing Aboriginal and treaty rights of the Aboriginal population of Canada" and defines Aboriginal Peoples as Status Indians, Metis, and Inuit. Those who drafted the Constitution in 1981 did not define what those existing rights actually were, so for past 30 years these rights have been clarified either through negotiation, through the courts, or through the recognition of past practice. Metis people in Ontario, for example, have recently won a superior court case establishing their right to hunt and fish on Crown-owned land in the province. People defined as Status Indians—although the preferred term in Canada is a member of a First Nation—possess certain rights because their ancestors agreed to treaties with the federal government many years ago, including federal government support for education and health care. In some provinces, First Nations fisheries exist because the government recognizes that they did not give up their right to fish on their land when the country was formed.

It has been argued that bestowing some groups special rights is a form of racism. Jim Pankiw, former Member of Parliament for Saskatoon-Humboldt, advances this claim as a central part of his political platform. Though he lost his seat in 2004, he has decided to run as an independent in the future elections. Controversy has swirled around Pankiw for several years, mainly about his views on Aboriginal peoples. At the 2009 press conference announcing his anticipated political comeback, Pankiw accused First Nations chiefs of racism for their continued advocacy of special rights on behalf of their people. A few years earlier a group of residents of Saskatoon filed a Human Rights Complaint against Pankiw on the grounds that he was wilfully promoting racism in pamphlets that were distributed out of his constituency office while he was an MP.

Is it racist, as Mr. Pankiw suggests, to provide groups with special rights in a society like ours that is otherwise committed to equality? Are Aboriginal rights a form of race-based preference that, as an image on Mr. Pankiw's website explains, puts "Whitey" at a disadvantage?

The issue of Aboriginal rights reflects processes of racialization, but Mr. Pankiw is wrong to suggest that recognizing Aboriginal rights is racist. To know why, we must look at the historical and social context. First, other categories of people also have certain group-based rights. Though it has proven to be not very effective, federal employment equity legislation aims to improve the employment prospects of people of colour, women, people with disabilities, *and* Aboriginal peoples. The rationale for this legislation when it was first crafted in 1986 was that members of these groups faced historical disadvantages in the Canadian labour market and that active measures needed to be taken to improve contemporary employment patterns. Providing people with certain group-based rights is not unprecedented in Canada, and these rights are perfectly compatible with the Canadian Charter of Rights and Freedoms.

Second, for the first one hundred or so years of Confederation, Status Indians did indeed possess some special rights. Many of these rights stemmed from treaties, in which the federal government had promised support for education and health care in exchange for land. But as well as certain rights, the Indian Act also imposed certain restrictions on Status Indians. Aboriginal peoples could not vote in federal elections until 1960; they could not move off reserves or travel without permission; they could not frequent pool halls and they could not consume liquor in public places. Government officials required categories to define Aboriginal peoples in order to enforce these combinations of rights and restrictions (Backhouse 1999).

The federal government designed the category of "Status Indian" or "Registered Indian." This legislation is over one hundred years old, and still largely in place today, with a list of Status Indians kept by authorities. When the register was first developed in the 1880s, as well as notions of blood and ancestry, the category of Status Indian also involved a degree of self definition: if people "lived like

Indians," and were accepted by Aboriginal communities, then they were placed on the list. Until 1985, non-Indian women who married Indian men were added to the list of Registered Indians, and so were their descendants. On the other hand, Indian women who married non-Indian men lost their status (they became defined as Non-Status Indians, or Metis). Their children also lost their Indian status (Frideres and Gadacz 2008).

In 1985 changes were made to address gender discrimination in the Indian Act. But those changes still left some gender discrimination in place. While the changes reinstated the Indian status of Indian women who married non-Indian men, and the status of their children, their grandchildren were still not allowed to claim Indian status. In a 2010 court case, the federal government was forced to change its rules and allow the grandchildren of women who lost their status to claim the identity of Indian (CBC 2010).

First Nation bands now have more power to define their own band membership. While the issue of the definition is complex, bands develop and regulate their own membership codes. Because band members have access to resources like housing, social assistance, and social services, bands must draw boundaries around who belongs to their community and who does not.

Bands have developed a number of models of group membership (Furi and Wherrett 2003), but those bands that use blood quantum rules have been the most criticized. The Kahnawake Mohawk community's code is probably the most controversial, in part because they are the most high-profile community to use this code (Lawrence 2004, 78). Culture and individual identity are also factors in Mohawk identity, but they seem to be subordinate to biological descent. As University of Victoria Professor Taiaiake Alfred notes, "Today there are many different ideas about what constitutes a Native person. We know what does not: pure self-identification and acting the part, however diligent the research or skilful the act" (Alfred 1999, 85).

Individuals in Kahnawake have lost jobs and have not been allowed to run for office because they have less than the requisite 50 percent blood quantum. In 1995 there were efforts to bar children from Kahnawake schools based on blood quantum (Lawrence 2004, 79).

Critics have argued that these kinds of membership codes are racist and in violation of basic human rights (Lawrence 2004, 78).

In defence of this kind of code, Alfred (1995, 174–77) argues that in the absence of an easily operational set of cultural criteria to define what being a Mohawk means, "Indian communities in the modern era have been forced to accept race-based criteria" (Alfred 1995, 174). This kind of racialized definition of group membership is "easy to police" because race can be readily measured. Alfred further argues that these criteria are the natural by-product of living in a racialized society with a racist history. Critics have argued that there is a double standard levelled at Mohawks when the blood quantum code is condemned. According to Lawrence (2004, 78), the Canadian government regularly uses blood quantum in its determination of resources eligibility in land claims settlements. Alfred admits that defining Mohawks by virtue of "blood" is a defensive reaction on the part of Mohawks faced with threats to their identity and to the future of their community. He identifies a number of specific threats, including: intermarriage with non-Mohawks; the wider popularity of assuming an Aboriginal identity; and individuals taking on an Aboriginal identity (and in some cases seeking formal reinstatement as Status Indians) who seek the special rights and monetary benefits associated with formal status.

"Membership," in Alfred's (1999, 85) view, "is a matter of blood and belonging determined through the institutions governing a community at a particular time." The problem, as we noted in Chapter 1, is that race is neither fixed nor obvious. In fact, it is very difficult to define race from a biological or blood quantum standpoint, and any definition will inevitably draw arbitrary boundaries between who belongs and who does not belong to a community.

Aboriginal History

The history of Aboriginal and European relations is messy, involving conflict, displacement, and forced integration. The injustices suffered by Aboriginal peoples include land taken without consent and communities relocated to clear the way for economic development or, in the north, to assert Canadian sovereignty. Additionally, treaty obligations have been reneged. A full history is impossible here. But it is worth considering how this history is grounded in racist attitudes imported from Europe, particularly that European culture was superior to that of Aboriginal peoples. Much of British and French colonial policy, and then later federal government policy, was based on assimilation as the most "humane" course of action (Titley 1986). Aboriginal peoples, it was widely believed, did not know what lay in their own best interests.

As European Canadian settlement grew and land became increasingly scarce, assimilation strategies intensified. The residential school system was introduced in the early 1880s. The rationale here was that children could be more easily assimilated into European Canadian society if they were separated from the influences of their families and cultures (Titley 1986). As we now know, much more went on in those schools than simply teaching Aboriginal children how to be European; many children were sexually and physically abused, and this abuse has had negative consequences not just for the survivors of that abuse but for the children and grandchildren of those who attended.

An early twentieth-century senior official in the Department of Indian Affairs wrote:

> It must not be forgotten … that we are working in a material that is stubborn in itself; the Indian constitutionally dislikes work and does not feel the need of laying up stores or amassing wealth. The idea which is ingrained in our civilization appears to be that a race must be thrifty and must surround itself with all matter of wealth and comforts before it is entitled to be considered civilized. The Indian has not yet reached that state, and it is doubtful he ever will—were such desirable. (Frank Pedley 1909; quoted in Miller 1996, 185–86)

Where children were sent to residential schools, plans were made to assimilate adult Aboriginal peoples. A strategy was devised in the late nineteenth century to encourage Native men and women to take up agriculture; this, it was felt, would lead to a more settled lifestyle, a greater sense of personal responsibility, and a capitalist work ethic. Hayter Reed, the head of Indian Affairs (1893–97), wrote:

> Corn precedes all civilization; with it is connected rest, peace and domestic happiness, of which the wandering savage knows nothing. In order to rear it nations must take possession of certain lands; and when their existence is thus firmly established, improvements in manner and customs speedily follow. They are no longer inclined for bloody wars, but fight only to defend the fields from which they derive their support. The cultivation of corn, while it furnishes man with a supply

of food for the greater part of the year, imposed upon him certain labours and restraints, which have a most beneficial influence upon his character and habits. (Quoted in Carter 1990, 15)

However, by the early twentieth century some Aboriginal peoples were becoming successful farmers with valuable land under their stewardship. Complaints to the Department of Indian Affairs about unfair subsidies led to the cessation of support for Aboriginal farming, denying requests—even by the Department's own farming instructors—to improve farming technology. The Department began to sell Native reserve land to Canadian farmers of European descent. A 1901 article in the Edmonton *Bulletin* reveals the prevailing view:

The Indians make no practical use of the reserves which they hold. Where the land is good and well situated for market white men can turn it to much better account than the Indians do. A township in a good hunting country and near a fishing lake is more valuable to the Indians than a township of fine agricultural land near a railway station. It is a loss to the country to have such lands lying idle in the hands of the Indians when white men want to use them and are willing to pay for them. It is a loss to the Indian to compel him to remain in uncongenial surroundings to which he cannot adapt himself when he has the opportunity to remove to congenial surroundings, and by the sale of the land ensure himself a comfortable annuity. (Quoted in Carter 1990, 245)

Other initiatives designed to assimilate Aboriginal peoples that did not involve scarce resources took hold. In the 1940s and 1950s, the Department of Indian Affairs encouraged the formation of homemakers' clubs for Aboriginal women on reserves. These clubs were designed to teach domestic skills like dressmaking, knitting, fruit preserving, and vegetable canning. They also organized lectures on health, nutrition, and child care (Edwards 2005). Although these were part of the overall assimilation project organized by the Department of Indian Affairs, Aboriginal women used these clubs to their own advantage, often taking control of the agendas of the clubs and shaping activities to suit their own interests rather than those of the federal government.

Over the course of the twentieth century, the Indian Act imposed special restrictions on Status Indians. In addition to the restrictions on voting, liquor consumption, and pool hall attendance, "pass" rules developed by the Department of Indian Affairs regulated the ability of Status Indians to leave their reserves, even for short periods of time. Permission was required to visit relatives on another reserve, to shop in town, even to sell eggs at a local market. Moreover, Status Indians were prohibited from hiring lawyers to help them with their land-related disputes with the federal government (Titley 1986). A great deal of the land that had been allocated to Status Indian communities through previous treaties was withdrawn and sold to European Canadians under less-than-transparent, or even illegal, circumstances.

These are only some of the examples of the oppression suffered by Aboriginal peoples. Though many of the more patronizing restrictions are gone, many today feel that the Indian Act continues to impose special restrictions on Status Indians, and as such is racist: band membership rules and band council decisions still have to be approved by the Department of Indian Affairs and Northern Development, and Aboriginal peoples on reserves are still prohibited from owning private property.

Resolving these cases of mistreatment is a complicated process. As with other communities around the world that have suffered at the hands of colonial governments, these historical wrongs live on into the present day. The conflict between members of Six Nations and residents of the community of Caledonia, Ontario, is probably a case study of both communities losing by government foot dragging. But settling these disputes does not have to be a zero-sum game. Creative solutions to decades-old disputes can be found, and can benefit both Aboriginal communities, and wider Canadian society. The year 2010 was the 10th anniversary of the signing of the Nisga'a Treaty, and it is widely regarded as a success story in the relationship between Status Indians and the federal government. As one Nisga'a leader explained, the treaty has "transformed B.C.'s Nisga'a Nation from beggars in their own lands to individual entrepreneurs who hold the keys to economic revival in northwest B.C." (Canadian Press 2010). When the Treaty was first signed, some politicians and residents of British Columbia called the agreement racist because it gave powers to people defined by descent (Taylor 1998/99). By most accounts, the sky has not fallen as a result of the negotiated settlement of the long-standing dispute over Nisga'a land. As philosopher Charles Taylor points out, the rhetoric of racism originally inhibited a complete understanding of the Treaty and its benefits for all residents of the province. Clearly, simplistic claims that such settlements are racist because they further confirm the existence of special rights for Aboriginal people need to be tempered by a more nuanced appreciation of the complex processes, shaped in part by racism, that have gotten us to this point.

Contemporary Conditions

Most people would remark that the standard of living is visibly different in Aboriginal reserves than in comparable communities in the rest of Canada. The visible differences are also evident in cities where Aboriginal people are concentrated in certain neighbourhoods. Reserve-based housing seems to be in poorer condition, cars and trucks seem older, streets are unpaved with few commercial businesses. Some parts of Canadian cities where Aboriginal people live have a similar range of problems: dilapidated houses, signs of substance abuse, prostitution, and gang violence (Totten 2009).

Unemployment rates in some reserve communities reach 70 or 80 percent. Unemployment rates for urban Aboriginal residents are lower than for reserve residents but still higher than those of non-Aboriginals. Earnings also reflect this disparity: Aboriginal peoples earn about 70 cents for every dollar earned by non-Aboriginal peoples (Greenaway 2010). Life expectancy is shorter, housing quality is poorer, and general measures of health and well-being are lower than for other Canadians. Aboriginal peoples are massively overrepresented in Canada's jails (Frideres and Gadacz 2008). Sociologist Mark Totten (2009) describes Aboriginal youth gang violence in western Canada as "epidemic."

At the same time, it is important to not paint too bleak a picture of Aboriginal lives in this country. Though there are disparities, some Aboriginal peoples of Canada are breaking out of poverty, staying in school longer, attaining higher levels of education, and attracting good jobs (Frideres and Gadacz 2008). One study found, for example, that Aboriginal women with a university degree earn nearly $2,500 more than non-Aboriginal women with a university degree (Wilson and Macdonald 2010). Economists Daniel Wilson and David Macdonald suggest that this earnings advantage may be because a high proportion of Aboriginal women with university degrees end up working in the public sector education jobs, which traditionally have high rates of unionization and good salaries.

But in spite of these advances, Aboriginal communities on the whole are less well off than the rest of Canada.

Racist explanations of Aboriginal conditions

Canadians have a long history of blaming Aboriginal peoples for their fate. Perhaps this is related to Canada's wealth and prosperity. Over the past two decades, the United Nations Human Development Index consistently ranks Canada as one of the best countries in the world to live (United Nations Development Program 2009). We have human rights legislation and a Charter of Rights and Freedoms, education, and health care. Social mobility is high. Waves of impoverished immigrants who came to Canada became successful socially and materially. Yet this overall wealth does not always extend to Aboriginal peoples.

The phenomenon that sociologists call "blaming the victim" takes many different forms, some of which are more sophisticated than others (Warry 2008). Here, there are stereotypes at work: substance abuse, welfare dependency, and laziness. The view here is that Aboriginal peoples cannot succeed because of a susceptibility to alcohol, a preference of welfare, and a culture that encourages laziness. There are academically respectable equivalents to each of these three stereotypes.

Richard Thatcher (2004) argues that the predominant explanation for First Nations peoples' alcohol abuse problems, which he describes colloquially as "the firewater theory," is a form of the disease model of alcoholism. Some physicians and medical researchers have attempted to document an apparent biological predisposition to alcohol abuse. For many years, the disease model of alcoholism was the predominant explanation of, and treatment for, alcohol abuse. At its simplest, in this model individuals who develop the disease of alcoholism are predisposed by brain chemistry. This dysfunction is reinforced and aggravated by extensive alcohol consumption. It is a chronic disease; managing it requires complete abstinence from alcohol. Thatcher argues that

> inherent in the firewater complex is the belief that aboriginal Canadians are constitutionally (genetically) incapable of moderation in the amount of alcohol they consume. … Drinking, moreover, is seen

as a social activity, typically carried out in venues devoted wholly to group drinking. It also tends to be carried out through binges, rather than as persistent, ongoing, addictive drinking. The firewater complex also includes the popular belief that "Indian drinking" is inevitably associated with extreme impairment and irresponsible and antisocial behaviour. The assumption is that, once a drinking episode has begun, indigenous North Americans lose their capacity to regulate their drinking behaviour, the amount they drink, as well as other behaviours during the episode. Colloquially stated, Indian drinking tends to quickly get "out of control." ... (2004, 130–31)

This approach to substance abuse in Native communities is incorporated into treatment programs. Thatcher argues that the thinking behind the "firewater complex" has been extended to explain many other social problems in reserve communities, including gambling, co-dependency, family violence, anxiety, depression, anger, and rage (Thatcher 2004, 139).

While, as Thatcher points out, brain chemistry or mental illness may play a role in individual cases, the very fact that the frequency of the problem varies so widely suggests that the social determinants of substance abuse are primary factors in its persistence (2004, 45). Thatcher argues that there is "no convincing evidence" that Aboriginal peoples "are genetically prone to alcohol problems or that they are necessarily problem drinkers if they do drink" (2004, 122). An alternative explanation sees problem drinking as the result of complex structural and historical factors stemming from the largely negative interactions with the dominant society. These factors include: the socialized patterns of learning about drinking within Aboriginal communities; the federal government's historical encouragement of dependency; the breakdown of social controls within communities to regulate anti-social drinking; and the absence of "stakes in sobriety" for many Aboriginal people (Thatcher 2004, 166–93). In other words, patterns of drinking are not rooted in an unalterable biology or culture, but rather in social conditions that produce certain kinds of cultural responses.

There is also a scholarly equivalent to the "lazy Indian" stereotype. The basic argument here is that Aboriginal cultures are inconsistent with success in a modern competitive capitalist environment. These arguments reappear every few years in different forms. In 1975 sociologist Mark Nagler argued that there was a cultural divide, in which the cultural characteristics in Aboriginal communities were at odds with the rest of Canada. A combination of factors are involved: mutual aid to family and community members is given freely without the expectation of return in money or in kind (18); wealth is not a symbol of prestige and success (19); "saving for future well-being, or delay of gratification for future benefit, is not a logical pattern of behaviour for Native Peoples" (20); Aboriginal culture has a present rather that future time orientation (21); and there is little tendency to place a monetary value on time (22). These factors combined help explain why Aboriginal people have high rates of unemployment, low incomes, and little investment in schooling as the pathway to success.

More recently, Frances Widdowson and Albert Howard (2008, 11) argue that at the time of contact, the "cultural gap" between Aboriginal peoples and Europeans "could not have been wider." Human cultural development can be classified by developmental stages—"savagery," "barbarism," and "civilization," corresponding to the three broad characterizations of cultures as Stone Age, Bronze Age, and Iron Age. According to Widdowson and Howard, Aboriginal peoples were in the Stone Age at the time of contact (or the Neolithic stage of cultural development) while Europeans were in the civilization stage (the Iron Age). This cultural gap persists today:

> A number of Neolithic cultural features, including undisciplined work habits, tribal forms of political identification, animistic beliefs, and difficulties in developing abstract reasoning, persist despite hundreds of years of contact. ... It is the persistence of these obsolete cultural features that has maintained the development gap, preventing the integration of many aboriginal peoples into the Canadian social dynamic. As in other courses such as the United States, Australia and New Zealand, the fast pace of capitalist development has made it difficult to incorporate hunters and gatherers and horticulturalists into modern economic processes. (Widdowson and Howard 2008, 13)

In other words, Aboriginal culture is ill equipped for modern civilized society. Widdowson and Howard's proposed solution is remarkably similar to those put forward one hundred years ago by government officials and missionaries: Canada must accelerate the cultural adaptation of Aboriginal peoples into Canadian society.

Another explanation involves the "welfare Indian" stereotype (Flanagan 2000). Instead of seeing Aboriginal culture as virtually unchanged over the past five hundred years since European contact, this model sees distortions as a result of misguided government policies. The cultural changes that have been directly and indirectly encouraged by years of government policies have restrained social and economic development. Economist John Richards (2005) argues that there is a welfare mentality, and government support and assistance has backfired, creating a culture of welfare dependency.

Some of these explanations are racist, and others racialized (without necessarily being racist). Scientists, doctors, addiction counsellors, and others who work within the framework of the disease model of alcohol and advocate what Thatcher calls the "firewater complex" are no doubt motivated by good intentions. Their search for a genetic basis for alcohol abuse may contribute to a racialized explanation of the problem, but there is no negative evaluation of the apparent genetic difference to qualify it as racist.

The other two explanations, however, not only define Aboriginal peoples as a collectivity in racialized terms, but they also negatively evaluate Aboriginal cultural difference. According to anthropologist Noel Dyck, repeated failures of Aboriginal policy rely on a "continuing racist belief that they [Aboriginal peoples] are 'actually' and, perhaps, innately inferior to whites" (Dyck 1991, 31). The argument that the government has distorted Aboriginal culture to create a welfare mentality places blame for the problem on an overly generous federal government and on Aboriginal peoples. This explanation brushes up against racism to the extent that even though it focuses on apparent government "generosity" as part of the problem, Flanagan also argues that differences in the degree of "civilization" of European and Aboriginal communities at the time of contact also play a key role. This implies that Aboriginal culture is stuck in a backward mode and has lacked the resilience to withstand the temptations of modern government generosity. The allegation that certain groups are unable to adapt to modern conditions is one of the old saws of traditional racist thinking.

Widdowson and Howard may be guided by good intentions. However, they portray Aboriginal cultures as essentially static, fixed and unchanging since European contact, and incapable of adapting to a competitive, market-based economy. Peter Kulchynksy argues that the language used by Widdowson and Howard sees culture, not race, as the source of the problem. The inferiority of Aboriginal peoples is not defined in terms of their apparent biology, but instead is defined in terms of their apparently inert culture. As we saw in Chapter 1, emphasizing culture instead of race does not render a given attitude free of racist overtones.

Racism as the explanation

An alternative explanation sees historical and contemporary racism, discrimination, and unequal treatment as the key to understanding Aboriginal difficulties.

Some argue that the overall treatment of Aboriginal peoples in Canada, and specifically the creation and operation of the residential schools, "was and continues to be nothing short of genocide" (Chrisjohn and Young 1995, 27). This is a controversial claim (see, for example, Neu and Therrien 2003), but clearly the historical mistreatment of Aboriginal peoples has led to many difficulties in the present.

The residential school experience is an example of the way that historical experiences of oppression can have an impact on present-day individuals and communities. Though residential schools began to close in the 1950s, the legacy of the system continues to have an impact today. "Residential school syndrome" is now seen to be responsible for many of the individual and social problems that Aboriginal peoples face. This refers to the intergenerational consequences of being taken from parents, and of not learning how to properly parent. As a result, personal pathological behaviour and family problems are explained as both the direct and indirect consequences of having attended these racist-inspired institutions.

In 2006 The Assembly of First Nations, along with representatives of Inuit communities, came to a settlement agreement over residential schools with the Government of Canada, the General Synod of the Anglican Church of Canada, the Presbyterian Church of Canada, the United Church of Canada, and Roman Catholic entities. The Indian Residential Schools Settlement Agreement, valued at $1.9 billion, provides for the establishment of an Indian Residential Schools Truth and Reconciliation Commission, an Aboriginal Healing Foundation, funding for commemorative projects, and common experience payments of $10,000 for the first year of attendance at a school and $3,000 per year for every year attended after the first year. Individuals may make claims for additional payments if they experienced physical or sexual abuse. The Assembly of First Nations operates a 24-hour hotline available for residential school survivors.

Time, of course, will tell whether these measures are enough to correct a history of racism directed toward Aboriginal peoples. Measures like these, including Prime Minister Stephen Harper's 2008 apology for the residential school system, do little, however, to address the current forms of racism that continue to place Aboriginal peoples at a disadvantage in this country. It is easier to blame contemporary problems on the past racism of the residential school system than it is to identify current policies and practices of Canadian society that keep Aboriginal peoples at a disadvantage.

Any serious effort to move forward needs to recognize that a long history of racist-inspired oppression cannot be erased overnight. Canadians must develop a better appreciation of the ways that the legacy of racism continues to impact life chances and experiences of Aboriginal peoples. Further, the damage that racism has caused Aboriginal individuals and communities cannot be solved simply through more government programs or through formal apologies. Aboriginal communities require re-empowerment in order to become fully functioning members of our national and international communities. This does not mean going back to some imagined "golden age" of life before European contact. It does involve imagining ways that Aboriginal peoples can retain their Aboriginal heritage and still be full participants in Canadian society.

Chapter 5

Policing

Many Canadians are familiar with the tragic story of Jane Creba, a 15-year-old girl killed by a stray bullet while shopping in downtown Toronto with her family on Boxing Day 2005. Fewer Canadians may recognize the name Chantal Dunn. Six weeks after Creba was killed, Dunn—a 19-year-old York University student—was shot and killed by a stray bullet while waiting for her boyfriend outside a community centre in Toronto. Creba's death sparked outrage in the city, and across the country more generally. The police mobilized to find and arrest those involved in the downtown shooting spree; by April 2010, four young men had been convicted of charges related to the shooting. However, to date, no charges have been laid in relation to the death of Chantal Dunn. Some media outlets in Toronto did cover this story, but overall there was far less public attention. Toronto did not "lose its innocence," as it was said to have done over the death of Jane Creba.

Is skin colour a factor in explaining the difference in police, public, and media reactions to these two murders? Chantal Dunn's mother believes this is the case. In a 2006 article in *The Toronto Star*, Dunn's mother asked "If my daughter was white, would anything be different?" (Henry and Huffman 2006). Police investigating the Dunn murder said no, but Dunn's mother—and she is not alone— maintains otherwise. The perception among those familiar with these two cases is that skin colour played a role in both media coverage and police reaction to the two crimes.

These two cases raise the question of a double standard in Canadian society, and within the police force more specifically. It has been argued that this double standard takes two forms. First the standard of policing is lower for black people, Aboriginal peoples, and other racialized groups, and particularly women from those groups. That is, police forces (and society more generally) do not take crimes against women of colour as seriously as crimes against other groups. Second, when black men and those from other ethnic groups are seen as the perpetrators of crime, they are over-policed; they are subject to extra scrutiny, earlier intervention, and harsher sentencing.

Under-Policing Aboriginal Women as Victims of Crime

In its report on violence and discrimination against Aboriginal women in Canada, a 2004 Amnesty International report found that Status Indian women between the ages of 25 and 44 were five times more likely than other Canadian women to die as a result of violence. The report stated that the police, and Canadian society more generally, are largely unconcerned about this high level of violence.

Aboriginal women confront racism on a number of levels. Given the legacy of colonialism and racism, dislocation and marginality are key factors: Aboriginal women suffer from high unemployment and poor educational opportunities. The legacy of the residential school and child welfare systems (which, for many years, placed Aboriginal children in non-Aboriginal adoption or foster care arrangements) is another factor. Blocked opportunities in the legitimate, mainstream economy coupled with inadequate role models and identity confusion from residential school and child welfare systems have forced numerous Aboriginal women into poverty. Many are forced to live on the street, suffer from substance abuse, and are drawn into the sex trade. These high-risk behaviours, so clearly an effect of the exclusion from mainstream Canadian society, make Aboriginal women vulnerable to violence from pimps, gangs, and those involved in the sex trade (Amnesty International Canada 2004).

The Native Women's Association of Canada's 2010 report *What Their Stories Tell Us: Research Findings from the Sisters in Spirit Initiative* suggests that there is a direct link between violence against Aboriginal women and the history of colonialism, present-day racism, and the socio-economic marginalization of Aboriginal women:

The experiences of violence and victimization of Aboriginal women do not occur in a vacuum. Violence is perpetuated through apathy and indifference toward Aboriginal women, and stems from the ongoing impacts of colonialism in Canada. While this process is rooted in history, the impacts of colonization continue to affect Aboriginal peoples, and perhaps more profoundly Aboriginal women, today. One example with regard to First Nations women is the administration of the Indian Act which has created ongoing barriers to citizenship for Aboriginal women and their children and the intergenerational impacts and trauma resulting from the residential school and child welfare systems. These are well known and documented patterns of historic, as well as contemporary colonization. Systemic racism and patriarchy has marginalized Aboriginal women and led to intersecting issues at the root of the multiple forms of violence. The result of the system of colonization is a climate where Aboriginal women are particularly vulnerable to violence, victimization, and indifference by the state and society to their experiences of violence. (Native Women's Association of Canada 2010)

Amnesty International similarly asserts that perpetrators of violence against Aboriginal women often justify, explain, and defend their actions by using racist ideas and dehumanizing ideologies:

It appears that some men seek out Indigenous women as targets for extreme acts of violence. These acts of violence against Indigenous women may be motivated by racism, or may be carried out in the expectation that society's indifference to the welfare and safety of Indigenous women will allow the perpetrators to escape justice. Impunity for such violence contributes to a climate where such acts are seen as normal and acceptable rather than criminal, and where women do not seek justice because they know they will not get it. (Amnesty International 2009, 2)

Testimonies at criminal trials paint a depressing picture of the attitudes toward Aboriginal women. The two young white men who were charged in the beating death of Pamela Dean George in Regina in 1995 are reported to have told an acquaintance that they had picked up an "Indian hooker," and that "she deserved it. She was an Indian" (Amnesty International Canada 2004, 46). It took 15 years for charges to be brought against two of the four men involved in the November 1971 murder of Helen Betty Osborne in The Pas, Manitoba. In the years immediately following Osborne's killing, the identities of the men who were responsible were apparently an open secret in The Pas. There is evidence that residents of the small northern Manitoba community considered the murder unimportant and did not pass on information that could have led to earlier arrests. The Manitoba Justice Inquiry established to look into this case and others concluded "that the community's silence was at least partly motivated by racism" (Amnesty International Canada 2004, 39).

Sociologists make a distinction between "deserving" and "undeserving" victims. Deserving victims are individuals or groups who experience some type of trauma or harm—such as starvation, murder, genocide. In the wrong place at the wrong time, deserving victims garner our support, sympathy, and concern. Undeserving victims, on the other hand, receive less of our compassion, sympathy, and understanding. The general public feels that such victims bring harm upon themselves through high-risk behaviour. They may also be too unlike "us" to garner significant support or empathy. In this way, there is often less sympathy when prostitutes, drug addicts, and others who live on the streets are victims of violence. This lack of compassion and care very often applies to Aboriginal peoples, who are seen to have chosen the high-risk behaviours that place them in vulnerable positions.

Furthermore, when Aboriginal women are victimized, there may well be less sympathy, not to mention less professionalism, from police and other justice-system authorities like prosecutors and judges. Grassroots Aboriginal and women's organizations, and the family members of victims of crime, are convinced that police, prosecutors, and judicial authorities treat these cases less seriously than cases in which white women are victims of crime.

There is considerable evidence of police indifference to cases involving Aboriginal women. Felicia Velvet Solomon's family reported the 16-year-old missing in Winnipeg in late March 2003. Her remains were found along the Red River a few months later. Solomon's family recounts the apparent indifference the Winnipeg police force displayed toward the investigation into their daughter's disappearance and death. Police inaction, the family felt, was influenced by the assumption that Felicia was either a prostitute or gang member, and that because the family was poor and Aboriginal, reports of Solomon's disappearance were not prioritized. One of Solomon's family members criticized this indifference publicly:

> When we listened to the news, when something happened to someone else's child, whether they are white or from any other kind of race or culture, they [the police] do everything. It's completely different when an Indian person goes missing. We see that. (Amnesty International Canada 2004, 61)

In the case of Pamela George, the Crown prosecutor told the jury that George "lived a life far removed from theirs," and they would have to consider the fact that she was a prostitute as part of the case. The judge agreed, and instructed the jurors to bear in mind that Ms. George "indeed was a prostitute" when they considered whether or not she had consented to sexual activity. The two young men were convicted of manslaughter and sentenced to six-and-a-half years in prison (Amnesty International Canada 2004). The case of Robert Pickton—the farmer who was convicted in 2007 of murdering and dismembering six women—raised wider concerns about Vancouver police during the late 1990s and early 2000s. Though Pickton was convicted of the second-degree murder of 6 women, he was also charged in the death of 20 others, which were stayed because he will serve the maximum sentence. The police had received many missing persons' reports of women working in the sex trade, but these reports were not given a high priority. According to one account, these women were seen as "inconsequential" (Travis 2006). One woman who escaped with multiple stab wounds testified against Pickton in 2003, but the charges were dropped since she was not considered an "effective witness" due to her criminal record and history of drug abuse (Matas 2010).

Today, a 720-kilometre stretch of Highway 16 between Prince George and Prince Rupert in northern British Columbia has been dedicated as a monument to missing women—it is called the Highway of Tears. Estimates of the number of women who have gone missing or been found murdered along the highway vary. Police say 18, but others say the number could be as high as 32. The vast majority of the missing and murdered women are Aboriginal. It was only when a young white woman, Nicole Hoare, disappeared while hitchhiking along that same stretch of highway in June 2002 that the police began to take the other disappearances more seriously. A special joint RCMP-Vancouver police unit is now probing violence against women along BC highways.

These cases point to a long-term pattern of indifference on the part of police. Groups like the Native Women's Association of Canada call for improved training and education of police officers and Canadians more generally about the history of colonialism, and present-day experiences of racism and discrimination. Amnesty International and the Native Women's Association of Canada have called for police forces to collect crime statistics based on the origins and identities of missing and murdered women. In particular, the 2004 Amnesty report is critical of police failure to collect information about the ethnicity of crime victims or missing persons when cases are entered into the Canadian Police Information Centre database. If this information is not collected, police have less ability to trace patterns of violence against at-risk groups. Yet, according to Amnesty,

> A number of police officers have told Amnesty International that they do not pay particular attention to the ethnic identity of victims of violent crimes because to do so would open them up to accusations of being "racist." To the contrary, the failure of police to identify and make public the full extent to which Indigenous women are victims of violent attacks helps perpetuate a profound and dangerous form of discrimination by denying public officials, other police officers and Indigenous women themselves the information necessary to expose and prevent such violence. The UN Human Rights Committee has asked Canada to explain why this information is not systematically gathered. (Amnesty International Canada 2005, 2)

Advocates argue that in addition to enabling police to make faster connections between cases, collecting this information would also raise awareness of Aboriginal women's disproportionate victimization in Canadian society. Collecting this information is not in itself racist, and for police to point to this as a concern fails to fully address the dangers faced by these at-risk populations.

Over-Policing: Racial Profiling

"White privilege" is a term used by sociologists and others to point to a metaphorical "invisible backpack" that provides a wide variety of hidden and unstated—but very real—social benefits (McIntosh 1988). White people rarely worry about being unfairly targeted by police as a result of their skin colour.

Much of the everyday world of policing involves exercising discretion. A police officer's job is to identify actual and potential crime. Police have some leeway in how they carry out their duties. Within limits, they decide what parts of a city to patrol. For minor infractions of the traffic or criminal code, they may lay a charge, write a ticket, or only give a warning. Police may at times also choose between informing a parent of minor infractions committed by their children or laying more serious charges. What role does racialization play in determining how police carry out their duties? In Canada this debate focuses mainly on whether young black men are subject to unfair and unwarranted police surveillance; this has been informally labelled as "driving while black."

Claims of unfair treatment of racialized groups at different levels in Canada's justice system is not new (see, for example, Backhouse 1999; Melchers 2006; Mosher 1998). Several task force reports, commissions of inquiry, and scholarly research papers have suggested that peoples of colour are both under-policed when they are victims of crime and over-policed when they are seen as perpetrators (see, for example, Commission on Systemic Racism in the Ontario Criminal Justice System 1995; Royal Commission on Aboriginal Peoples 1996a). More recently, public attention and academic debate have focused on racial profiling, particularly among black and Aboriginal communities (Henry and Tator 2010; Tanovich 2006).

There is no agreement on how racial profiling should be defined. Criminologist Ron Melchers suggests that the most influential definition on Canadian jurisprudence is offered by the African Canadian Legal Clinic:

> Racial profiling is criminal profiling based on race. Racial or colour profiling refers to that phenomenon whereby certain criminal activity is attributed to an identified group in society on the basis of race or colour resulting in the targeting of individual members of that group. In this context, race is illegitimately used as a proxy for the criminality or general criminal propensity of an entire racial group. (Quoted in Melchers 2006, 24)

In Canada, the statistical evidence in relation to racial profiling comes from two widely publicized—and controversial—studies. The first, conducted by the *Toronto Star* in 2002, showed that black Torontonians are over-represented in certain charge categories, and that black offenders are treated more harshly following arrest and are much more likely to be held in custody for bail hearings than their white counterparts. *The Star* contends that these patterns are upheld even when other relevant legal factors have been taken into account (Rankin et al. 2002; Wortley and Tanner 2003, 1).

The second study, conducted by University of Toronto criminologist Scott Wortley at the request of the Kingston, Ontario, chief of police, found that black people are 4 times more likely to be pulled over by police, and Aboriginal peoples are 1.4 times more likely. The study also found that 40 percent of black males between the ages of 15 and 24 were stopped by police during the study year, compared to 11 percent of their white counterparts. Some 10 percent of the stops involving a black person resulted in an arrest or charge compared to 6 percent for white individuals (Wortley 2005).

A second approach to collecting information on racial profiling asks peoples of colour about their perceptions of the justice system (Solomon and Palmer 2004). In one of its surveys, the 1995 Commission on Systemic Racism in the Ontario Criminal Justice System found that 43 percent of black male residents of Toronto reported having been stopped by police in the previous two years; this was true of only 25 percent of white male residents and 19 percent of Chinese male residents. It also found that "there were widespread perceptions among black, Chinese and white Torontonians that judges discriminate on the basis of race" (1995, 178). In 2003, 36 black police officers were asked to recount their experiences of racial profiling; a majority reported being stopped and questioned when off-duty by other police officers "for no other reason than the colour of their skin" (Tanovich 2006, 1–2).

David Tanovich is one of Canada's leading lawyers dealing with cases of racial profiling. In his book *The Colour of Justice*, Tanovich (2006, 1) argues that the colour of justice in Canada is white: "If you are not White, you face a much greater risk of attracting the attention of law enforcement officials in public spaces such as the highway, street, border, or airport." Tanovich offers two important observations. First, the many examples of racial profiling show that increased surveillance is not a result of particular individual behaviour, but rather of appearance. Second, day-to-day racial profiling is primarily about stereotyping rather than the expression of overt racism. Racial profiling can be conscious or unconscious. In the case of the police, officers focus on those components of the profile corresponding with pre-existing assumptions and organize their behaviour accordingly.

These studies have been controversial. When the 2002 *Toronto Star* study was published, Julian Fantino, then chief of police in Toronto, famously said: "We do not do racial profiling. We do not deal with people on the basis of their ethnicity, their race, or any other factor. We're not perfect people but you're barking up the wrong tree. There's no racism" (*Toronto Star* 2002). Some social scientists have also questioned the evidence on which allegations of racial profiling are based (Harvey 2003; Melchers 2006). In turn, others argue that denying racial profiling is another indication of the strength of racism in Canada (Henry and Tator 2010).

In a study of policing and profiling, my colleague William Shaffir and I (2009) found that these two views of racial profiling may not be mutually exclusive. Instead, we found that the disagreement depends a great deal on definitions. Police do not in fact deny using profiling in the course of their work. But many make a distinction between racial profiling and criminal profiling. One police officer explains that his work depends on profiling, but not linked solely to race or culture:

> As police officers, we are trained in certain ways, and then you build instincts. Because when we're out on the street, we rely on our instincts. We are trained investigators in the sense that we need to do profiling. And what kind of profiling is that? Criminal profiling. It has nothing to do with racial profiling. … We profile criminals. We do geographic profiling. It assists us to identify our problems and localize them and address them. When we go out … we do not target any specific culture or race. However, if we do come into a problematic area, and we start to ply our trade—policing—then if they happen to fall within those parameters, there's not much we can do. (Quoted in Satzewich and Shaffir 2009)

In effect, if the "criminal" turns out to be a person of colour, it is due to the ethnic landscape of the urban environment and not to overt racial profiling of a given ethnic group. This perspective is supported by a black officer, who was very sensitive to the claims that racial profiling is endemic to policing. He stressed the necessity to distinguish between profiling in general and racial profiling in particular:

> We talk about racial profiling in our office, and with our officers, and we say to a certain extent profiling exists in policing and you need it to some extent, but you have to recognize you can't label everyone, you know. You can say that I find stolen autos on the east mountain, for example, OK, so are you saying that all people that live on the east mountain steal cars? That's not a realistic a + b = c knowledge. ... If I want to go look for stolen cars, ya, I might go look toward the east mountain. But it doesn't mean that's always the case and all people on the east mountain steal cars. ... A certain amount of profiling does exist in policing. It has to exist. (Quoted in Satzewich and Shaffir 2009)

While the distinction between criminal profiling and racial profiling may seem subtle to those outside of policing, it is clear in the minds of police officers. The police argue that to carry out their work effectively they need to use a certain amount of "instinct" and their overall experience of criminality. As well, they need an accumulated knowledge of neighbourhoods that involves assessments of a range of cues about appearance, dress, and demeanour, among other factors.

The Consequences of Racial Profiling

In 2003 the Ontario Human Rights Commission carried out a study into the human costs of racial profiling. Its mandate was broad in scope and not limited to police profiling. The Commission placed ads in a number of English and French language newspapers and contacted over one thousand individuals and organizations to encourage Ontarians to submit their comments and experiences. Over eight hundred responses were received; roughly half were specifically about racial profiling. In six days of public hearings in May and June 2010, the Commission des droits de la personne et des droits de la jeunesse also conducted its own study into the experiences of racial profiling in Quebec. The Quebec Commission heard from panels of experts, but also received 150 submissions from members of the public who shared their experiences of racial profiling (Commission des droits de la personne et des droits de la jeunesse 2010).

Though the full report of the Quebec Commission is yet to be released, their study and the Ontario Human Rights Commission report provide glimpses into the experiences and consequences of racial profiling, although in both cases the authors themselves agree that it is by no means a random sample. The Quebec Commission recounted the story of a mother who explained the experiences of her young son.

> My 15-year-old son was playing hockey in an alley near our home in Outremont, like he always does. I gave him an 8:00 p.m. curfew. During the game, a police car pulled up and motioned for my son to approach the car. The police officers asked him a number of questions, including his name, the name of his school, and the names of his parents. My son is mulatto. They asked him which one of his parents was Black.
>
> When he replied that his mother was black, one of the police officers said "that's not a Haitian name!" They asked him what he wanted to be when he grew up, and he told them that he wanted to be a lawyer. Then they asked him "What do you have against the police force?" My son explained that he had nothing against them, but that he wanted to be a lawyer and that he had to go because it was nearly 8:00 p.m. and his parents had given him a curfew.
>
> He told us about it the next day. We went to the police station three days later. We were told that this is how they do their job. They call it "getting close to the people".
>
> Strangely, my son was the only "visible" minority among his group of friends, and he was the one who was questioned without reason. He wasn't dressed "yo", but in sportswear, like the others. (Commission des droits de la personne et des droits de la jeunesse 2010)

The Ontario Commission reported that some of the most profound negative effects of profiling were on children and youth, particularly in their interactions with the police and the educational system. In relation to experiences with police, one young man explained that

> even if I am standing in a MTHA [Metro Toronto Housing Authority] area with another university student and cops pass I always stop

and look to make sure that I am not being challenged by the cops. It's a feeling of fear, and of being less than them as they are in an authoritative position. We shouldn't be afraid of people who are supposed to be protecting our rights. (Ontario Human Rights Commission 2003, 24)

The Commission reported that individuals who were subject to racial profiling often distrust the police, and this may contribute to difficulties in police recruitment of members of different communities. Two submissions to the Commission summarize a discomfort with police authority:

Profiling does nothing but create distrust and resentment when it is done. This in turn causes a negative backlash in the community. This is part of the reason that the police force gets very little cooperation when dealing with the Black community. If a person does not feel valued by the system, you will in turn see how that person can become a negative force.

   People are afraid to talk to the police in the Black community. ... There are good cops, but the bad ones make us mistrustful of all police. It makes it hard for them to solve crime. (Ontario Human Rights Commission 2003, 27)

Individuals also reported modifying their own behaviour as a result of profiling. While most parents worry about what happens to their children when they are out at night, many black parents have an extra layer of fear. Some instruct their children to stay home at night, to avoid driving in certain nice areas of town lest they be mistaken for a criminal, and to avoid driving expensive cars for fear of being accused of theft.

It is worth noting that some social scientists feel that such studies are of limited use. They argue that studies by the Ontario Human Rights Commission and others are biased (Melchers 2006). Criminologist Ronald-Frans Melchers argues that there is another side to the consequences of racial profiling: he doubts that police regularly engage in racial profiling in Canada, and worries instead that repeated allegations—based on poor supporting evidence—heightens social tensions and divisions, and creates further mistrust of police within racialized communities. Black and other young people of colour may consequently interpret their interactions with police as forms of racial profiling, which in turn leads to greater distrust. As Melchers explains,

> Racial profiling beliefs are a problem in and of themselves which, however they come to be held, serve to further alienate black and other visible minority people from mainstream Canadian society and reinforce perceptions of discrimination and racial injustice. Racial profiling beliefs facilitate a culture of entitlement, disrespect and lawlessness, especially among young men, that places them at greater risk. These beliefs also render visible minority people more vulnerable to crime and disorder by driving a wedge between their communities and law enforcement. While there are those among groups advocating for belief in "racial profiling" who see such developments as politically useful tools for recruitment to their cause or to enlist support for further claims of measures favouring asymmetrical rights, the consequences of such advocacy are pernicious and widespread in their effects and threaten equality before and respect of the law, as well as public safety. (Melchers 2006, 22)

This chapter has highlighted how members of the Aboriginal and black communities in Canada believe that they are treated unfairly by the police and justice system authorities, attaching racial meanings to their interactions with police. The general level of apathy on the part of society and some police forces to the violence experienced by Aboriginal and other racialized women strongly suggests that their victimization has historically not been taken as seriously as the victimization of other groups. Aboriginal women should not be seen as "undeserving victims," and certainly not treated by police as disposable because of their often marginal positions in our society.

Racial profiling is an extraordinarily divisive issue in Canada. As we noted in the Introduction, no one in Canada wants to be labelled a racist, or be accused of discrimination. This is particularly true of the police, who rely on public trust and respect in order to effectively carry out their work. Where to draw the line between legitimate criminal profiling and illegitimate racial profiling continues to be a matter of contention. The way police take race into account should depend on the context. Given that the victimization of Aboriginal women is intimately connected to historical and present-day racism, it seems appropriate for the police to consider background as a factor. In other words, the police need to racialize their understanding of the context within which Aboriginal women are victimized. The other side of the coin, however, is much more complicated. When it comes to the racialization of perceived offenders, police argue that skin colour and perceived race and ethnicity may be only two of the many factors that they consider when doing their work. In other words, some say that racialization is part of policing. Yet, many critics argue that any process of racialization of perceived offenders is inherently racist. Both sides of this debate are compelling, but perhaps one way to reconcile the two positions is to consider what turns racialized policing into racist policing.

Chapter 6

Islamophobia

A New Racism?

The hijackers who flew airplanes into the World Trade Center and the Pentagon on September 11, 2001, did Muslims around the around the world few favours. Already many westerners felt some discomfort with Islam as a result of Ayatollah Ruhollah Khomeini's 1989 fatwa against Salman Rushdie for writing *The Satanic Verses*. Judged to be a blasphemy against Islam, the publicly issued fatwa offered $2.5 million to anyone who killed Rushdie or those involved with the book's publication (Hitchens 2009); Rushdie survived by going into hiding, but the book's Japanese translator was killed in 1991. The same year saw attacks on the book's Italian translator and its Norwegian publisher. Several bookstores in England carrying *The Satanic Verses* were bombed. Rushdie has since come out of hiding, but the fatwa against him has never been formally withdrawn. While Edward Said (1979) argues that there has been a long-standing fear of Islam within Western culture, the "Rushdie affair," as it came to be known, arguably marked a turning point in those fears: the "holy war" had come to the streets of London, New York, and other Westernized cities (Hitchens 2009).

The events of September 11, 2001, marked another turning point, provoking a new wave of fear of Islam (Razack 2008). These attacks were undertaken in the name of Islam, and the target was America. For some, 9/11 was an attack against an entire society's political and economic system, its values, and larger way of life. Samuel Huntington, the American political scientist and one-time advisor to the George W. Bush administration, suggested that the attacks were proof that the world is heading toward a "clash of civilizations" (Huntington 2006). Since 2001, the issues of terrorism and national security topped Americans' list of most pressing policy priorities; only in 2008–9 did the worldwide economic collapse replace terrorism and national security as Americans' top policy concern (Pew Research Center for People and the Press 2009).

Has Islam replaced Communism as the new enemy of the West? Such enemies, the theory goes, are needed to bring societies together, to create solidarity, and perhaps more importantly, to justify the buildup of military power. Following Communism's collapse in the early 1990s, Islam—by design or default—may have started to play this role in the Western imagination. This threat can justify the spread of American influence abroad and continued investment in the military industrial complex. The website Islamophobia-watch. com (n.d.) describes Islamophobia "as a racist tool of Western Imperialism. ..."

The deliberate construction of Islam as a new enemy of the West, replacing Communism, sounds hyper-conspiratorial. Certainly there is no shortage of conspiracy theories about the true motives and real forces behind September 11. However, there is little question that Islam and Muslims have at some level become the West's new "other." Murad Qureshi, a city councillor in London, England, said recently, "Muslims have become the new political Black" (Commission on British Muslims and Islamophobia 2004, 3). Though Islam is a religion, many commentators nevertheless suggest that as a result of the September 11, 2001, attacks, Muslims have been subject to increasing levels of racism in Canada and around the world (Arat-Koc 2006).

Muslims and Islam

Although Islam is the second-largest religion worldwide, many confess to know very little about its practices and its followers. Some common misconceptions construe the fundamental truths of Islam, many of which are shared with the Judeo-Christian tradition. For example, being Muslim is not an indication that someone is a descendent of people from the Middle East. In fact, only 20 percent of Muslims are Arab; the majority are African or Asian. Just like any other religion, there are a number of sects within the religion. Unfortunately, the sects of Islam are often lumped together by outsiders, and unlike Christianity or Judaism, the actions of the few are associated with the many. In fact, extremism is not conducive to the aims of Islam: the name "Islam" means "peace and submission to God."

As Judaism, Christianity, and Islam are all monotheistic, it might be confusing for Muslims to hear non-Muslims speak of Allah (literally "God") as a different God than Christians and Jews worship. To followers of Islam, Christians, Jews, and Muslims are all part of the same religious family, and there are different traditions and histories. Just as Christians believe Jesus and the Bible supersede Moses and the Old Testament, Muslims believe that the Quran is God's most recent revelation to the Prophet Muhammad. The Quran shares the belief in Satan, divine judgement, and moral responsibility, among others.

Sunni and Shia, the two major divisions of Islam, differ in the way that they choose their elders. Sunnis, the 85 percent majority who are often considered "orthodox," believe that religious scholars should become religious leaders, or caliphs. Shiites believe in blood lineage, and one can only claim to be an imam if they are a descendent of the Prophet's family.

Where Islam differs from the other monotheistic religions is in its practices. The five pillars of the Islamic faith are the following: faith, prayer, almsgiving, discipline, and pilgrimage to Mecca. A misconception that has grown in years since September 11, 2001, is the inclusion of jihad in these pillars. Jihad is not the sixth pillar in the way non-Muslims perceive it—it literally means "to struggle" in the path of God, as did the Prophet Muhammad and his early companions. Just as extremists would in any other religion, Muslim extremists have interpreted the meaning of their holy text to serve an agenda. In the case of jihad, it has become a justification for "holy war," but this is a far cry from what most Muslims believe.

Carleton University Professor Karim Karim's (2009) study *Changing Perceptions of Islamic Authority among Muslims in Canada, the United States and the United Kingdom* examines how "lay" Muslims understand Islam and Islamic authority. Karim finds that many Muslims are not simply followers of their respective religious authorities, but instead actively participate in the process of defining for themselves and their families what constitutes an "authentic" Muslim. He quotes an American Muslim woman on the subject of authority:

There are a lot of things now, personally, when I'm trying to make a decision about something where I don't care what the scholars say.

I don't care if the scholars say I should fast when I'm pregnant, or it's not okay to pay for the days you missed for your period, even if you're pregnant or breastfeeding for six years. ... I know when it comes to some issues like women, *fiqh* [Islamic jurisprudence] is so flawed. (Quoted in Karim 2009, 19)

Furthermore, in the same way that many Roman Catholics and Anglicans criticize, respectively, the Pope and the Archbishop, Karim notes that many Muslims criticize their imams. For example, some Muslims feel that imams—who in North America and Britain are often relatively recent immigrants—have too little knowledge of "real world" issues. Karim notes that some Muslims express frustration over the advice given by their religious leaders on how to be Muslim in the modern world, when the leaders themselves may know little of daily life. As one of Karim's focus group interviewees in Montreal explained,

My ultimate fantasy would be to find an imam who gives a *khutbah* (sermon) in a Friday mosque who happens to be someone who goes out to work from nine to five, takes the bus, is dealing with his kid who is picking up a marijuana joint. ... This is the kind of person that I want instructing me on Friday, not speaking to me about the battles that we won 1,200 years ago. (Quoted in Karim 2009, 10)

Muslims are diverse in terms of their beliefs about religious authority and engagement with modern life. As with other major world religions, believers interpret sacred texts and religious authority in different ways. There are degrees of orthodoxy in all world religions: not all Jews are kosher, not all Sikhs wear turbans, and many Roman Catholics practice birth control. For some people their religious faith embodies the sacred belief that the purpose of life is to serve God. For others, religion may still be closely connected to their identity even when they do not believe in God or practice the rituals associated with Hinduism, Judaism, or Christianity.

Further, the practice of Islam is also shaped by local cultural traditions and expectations. Amani Hamdan writes in her study of Arab Muslim women in Canada,

Although the *Quran* and *Sunna* (the sayings and actions of the Prophet Muhammad) are foundational resources of Islamic tenets, there is no single definitive interpretation of each or of both. Muslims do not have a single definitive interpretation of these sacred texts, and … this lack of a sole divine interpretation is attributed to the flexibility of Islam as a faith. In other words, the absence of a definite interpretation of the Islamic divine texts means that Muslims are encouraged to interpret … [the] texts in light of contemporary contexts. (2009, 206)

Hamdan suggests that the interpretation of the Quran and other texts is shaped by economic and political factors, in addition to the wider customs, culture, and traditions of given societies. She suggests that what sometimes appears to be prescription for acceptable social behaviour stemming from Islam may in fact be a reflection of local cultural histories. Thus, practices like the prohibition of girls' education and female genital mutilation in some countries where Islam is the majority religion are not necessarily prescribed by Islam, but local traditions (Hamdan 2009, 52; von der Osten-Sasken and Uwer 2007).

The current debate about wearing the hijab or niqab reflects the diversity of Islam. Some Muslims interpret this as a religious obligation; for others it is a cultural expression. Political Scientist Christian Joppke further suggests that Muslim women attach different meanings to head and face covering. For some, particularly first-generation immigrant women, it is a symbol marking their identity of origin. For others—especially second-generation young Muslim women who are expected to wear a veil by their parents—the veil is part of a transition to modernity. It allows them to take part in public life in the West, including attending higher education: it has the potential for liberation from traditionally defined roles. For others, wearing a veil is a symbol of autonomy and of resistance to racism and Islamophobia (Joppke 2009, 12–13).

Most Muslims observe their Islamic faith peacefully, respectfully, and non-violently, but extremists exist everywhere. This is true of Islam as much as of Christianity, Judaism, and other world religions. The Christian identity movement in the United States, for example, is a loosely knit group of ultra-conservative white supremacists. Some contend that the Bible predicts an upcoming race war in which they will be the last line of defence of the white race. Obviously, most Christians interpret the Bible very differently. Islam is no more or no less violent than any other religion; what matters are different interpretations.

Islamophobia

At first blush, it seems odd to describe Islamophobia as a form of racism. After all, as we defined the term earlier in this book, racism involves the negative evaluation of groups defined and constructed by reference to their perceived biological makeup and/or physical appearance. It is about the social construction and social evaluation of physical differences like skin colour and presumed race. But as we also discussed earlier, racism has taken on new forms. Today, code words and seemingly neutral language are sometimes used to express negative attitudes toward a group. These code words allow individuals or organizations to discriminate against a given group, and at the same time allow them to deny that they are racist. As a result, the former criticisms sometimes stand in for racially based criticisms.

The term Islamophobia first came into widespread use in Britain in the 1990s. Even before the attacks of September 11, 2001, sections of British society were concerned about the apparent rise in Islamophobia in that country. Sparked in part by the negative treatment of Muslims in Britain as a consequence of the Rushdie affair, an organization called The Runnymede Trust—a think tank mandated to deal with matters of ethnic and racial equality and justice—issued a report in 1997 titled *Islamophobia: A Challenge for Us All*. The Trust made a distinction between what it called closed and open views of Islam (see Table 6-1).

The Runnymede Trust report characterized closed views of Islam as "Islamophobia." In a follow-up report, Islamophobia was specifically defined as a form of racism. The report suggested that the definition of racism required expansion

> to refer to a wide range of intolerance, not just to intolerance where the principal markers of difference is physical difference and skin colour. For example, the term should encompass patterns of prejudice and discrimination such as antisemitism and sectarianism, where the markers of supposed difference are religious and cultural rather than to do with physical appearance. ... There are clear similarities between antisemitism, sectarianism, and Islamophobia, and between these and other forms of intolerance. The plural term "racisms" is sometimes used to evoke this point. (Commission on British Muslims and Islamophobia 2004, 12)

Table 6-1 Closed and Open Views of Islam

Distinctions	Closed Views of Islam	Open Views of Islam
Monolithic/diverse	Islam is seen as a monolithic bloc, static and unresponsive to change.	Islam is seen as diverse and progressive, with internal differences, debates, and development.
Separate/interacting	Islam is seen as separate and "other." It does not have values in common with other cultures, is not affected by them, and does not influence them.	Islam is seen as interdependent with other faiths and cultures. It has certain shared values and aims, it is affected by them, and enriches them.
Inferior/different	Islam is seen as inferior to the West. It is seen as barbaric, irrational, primitive, and sexist.	Islam is seen as distinctively different, but not deficient, and as equally worthy of respect.
Enemy/partner	Islam is seen as violent, aggressive, threatening, supportive of terrorism, and engaged in a "clash of civilizations."	Islam is seen as an actual or potential partner in joint cooperative enterprises and in the solution of shared problems.
Manipulation/sincere	Islam is seen as a political ideology and is used for political or military advantage.	Islam is sen as a genuine religious faith practiced sincerely by its adherents.
Criticism of West defended/considered	Criticisms made of the West by Islam are rejected out of hand.	Criticisms of the West and other cultures are considered and debated.
Discrimination defended/criticized	Hostility towards Islam is used to justify discriminatory practices towards Muslims and exclusion of Muslims from mainstream society.	Debates and disagreements with Islam do not diminish efforts to combat discrimination and exclusion.
Islamophobia seen as natural/problematic	Anti-Muslim hostility is seen as natural or normal.	Critical views of Islam are themselves subjected to critique, lest they are inaccurate and unfair.

Source: Commission on British Muslims and Islamaphobia 1997

In the British political context, this broadened definition of racism was used to justify the inclusion of discrimination against Muslims within the wider purview of the country's Race Relations legislation. Until 2003, British legislation did not prohibit discrimination based upon religion, which left many within the Muslim community "with little faith in the race industry" (Commission on British Muslims and Islamophobia 2004, 13).

Some social scientists argue that defining Islamophobia as a form of racism may stretch the definition of the term too far (Miles and Brown 2003); this disagreement will most likely continue (Arat-Koc 2006). What is clear, however, is that Muslims have become targets of hostility and discrimination in Canada and in other countries around the world. Let us examine some of the forms that this has taken in this country.

Muslims as "The New Political Black"

In many Western countries, one of the areas of public life where Islamophobia has surfaced most often is crossing borders, either among visitors to other countries or permanent residents. The term "flying while Muslim" captures this new form of discrimination. Many of the public debates about immigration in Western countries in the 1980s and 1990s focused on black immigrants, particularly Caribbean and African immigrants, and their perceived failure to fully integrate into British society. These immigrants were defined as problem populations threatening the stability of British society. In other Western European countries at the same time, debates about "third-world" migrants were largely coded terms for black immigration; many countries regarded this issue with alarm. The 1986 Single European Act was intended to help facilitate the free movement of goods, services, and people within the European Union and to further strengthen border control measures into Europe. But critics claimed that the major intent of the legislation was to keep black immigrants out of Europe. According to a Manchester, England, immigrant aid association,

> What it will mean for black people is not freedom of movement but its opposite. It will mean the establishment of a "Fortress Europe" in which they will have no part except as a rigidly controlled work force ... the main issue being confronted by the EC in opening the borders

is how to close them to black people, not to lose their labour but to control it along with their lives. (Quoted in Miles 1993, 212)

As we have seen, moral panic about the negative consequences of immigration is nothing new. The demonization of black immigration in the 1980s and 1990s also occurred in Canada, focused on black immigration in general, and immigrants from Jamaica in particular. Frances Henry and Carol Tator (2010) argue that the Canadian media tended to "Jamaicanize" crime, pointing to the apparent over-representation of Jamaicans in criminal ranks.

Muslims more recently have nudged black people aside and have moved up the list of "risk" groups. While the debate about "reasonable accommodation in Quebec" in 2008 and 2009 was ostensibly related to a variety of religious and ethnic communities, much of the concern was really about Muslims, and the apparently unreasonable demands they were placing on Quebec society.

There is considerable evidence behind the perception that Arabs and Muslims are targeted when they cross international borders, including the border into this country. In a 2007 survey, 22 percent of respondents reported that Border Services Officers do not treat all travellers equally. Of this 22 percent, almost half reported that the Canada Border Services Agency used racial, ethnic, and/or religious profiling (EKOS Research Associates 2007, 91, 94).

In 2008 a University of British Columbia Faculty of Law research group conducted a study on the impact of racial profiling of Muslims in Canada. Like the Ontario Human Rights Commission study (see p. 78–80), the research was particularly interested in exploring the consequence for Muslims of September 11, 2001. They conducted a small number of face-to-face interviews with Muslim Canadians who reported that their experiences of profiling mainly took place during international airplane travel. In terms of the personal consequences of profiling, one interviewee explained,

You are ripping someone apart not because they're a bad person but because of the colour of their skin or where they were born and raised. … Canada has treated me for the most part, very well. I think people will get it that we're part of this community, part of this society and there's more to people of Muslim background than what you see on TV. (Gova and Kurd 2008, 30)

The study also revealed that some interviewees engage in what they called "self-censorship" of their religious identities and practices in order to avoid police profiling, or profiling by other security forces. In other words, they de-emphasize aspects of their religious or cultural identity when crossing borders. Some spoke with resignation; profiling was simply part of the "new normal." Those interviewed also spoke of how this kind of profiling affected the operations of charities and cultural institutions. Individuals associated with charities and other organizations felt particularly vulnerable to charges of being non-Canadian, or labelled as a terrorist or terrorist supporter. One respondent who works with international humanitarian organizations explains:

> [A] climate of fear that exists within these organizations. ... I make sure there's absolute fiscal transparency to ensure that every single penny is accounted for. We have to ensure that no one on the board has any religious affiliation. ... [W]e cannot form an organization that helps needy people in Afghanistan or Iraq but not have anyone on the board that has religious [affiliation]—without basically kick[ing] the Imam off one of the boards that I'm on. ... (Gova and Kurd 2008, 38)

The consequences of profiling at borders seem to also spread into the wider economy. Reem Bahdi's (2003) analysis of stereotyping Muslims as potential terrorists found that Arab employers in Windsor refused to hire Arab employees, or even "Arab-looking" employees out of fear that they were more likely to be stopped and detained when crossing the border (Bahdi 2003, 309–310); as a result, some Arab employers hired mostly white workers. Bahdi also analyzes how lost and ruined reputations are another part of the psychological costs of racial profiling (309).

Bahdi characterizes Muslim profiling as a counterproductive policing strategy. Rather than enhancing security, this kind of profiling leads to increased distrust of authority figures, even when individuals do nothing wrong. It sends a message to Muslims that they are not fully Canadian; the result is that profiled individuals may be less likely to interact with the justice system, less inclined to seek remedies if in need.

The point is that if the laws, policies, and practices that are in place to reach the professed end of fighting terrorism are perceived as ineffective and unjust, then individuals who hold such perceptions will be less likely to turn to them. Justice, as the old adage goes, must not only be done, but must be seen to be done. (Bahdi 2003, 311)

Muslims and the Media

After it became clear that the terrorist attacks of September 11 had been carried out in the name of Islam, leaders of many Western governments appealed for calm. There was an upsurge in attacks in Canada, the United States, and elsewhere against Muslims and others who were mistaken for Muslims. A Hindu temple in Hamilton, Ontario, was burned; police believe the attackers mistook the temple for a mosque. In the US, Muslims and people mistaken for Muslims were assaulted. Mosques were vandalized.

Political leaders in the two countries publicly came out in defence of their resident Muslim populations, pointing out that the vast majority of Muslims were peaceful citizens who condemned the attacks as much as did non-Muslims. Leaders warned against vigilante-type retaliation against their Muslim neighbours. Shortly after the attacks, Prime Minister Jean Chrétien visited a Mosque in Ottawa, and George W. Bush visited a mosque in Washington DC, to show support for Muslim communities (Zia n.d.).

Despite these appeals for calm, however, governments have contributed to the perception that Muslims are inherently prone to terrorism through their apparent sanctioning of extra vigilance over Muslims who cross international borders. The media is also implicated. A 2000 study of press images over a 10-year period between 1972 and 1982 found that Arabs were portrayed in the Canadian media as "irrational, backward, bloodthirsty, amoral and ignorant" (Bullock and Jafri 2000). In the aftermath of the events of September 11, 2001, "terrorist" was added to this list and "Arabs" morphed into "Muslims."

Many of the debates about Islamophobia in Canada, and in the West more generally, take place in the context of media representations of Muslims. Controversies have generated significant public debates about the meaning of hate speech, Islamophobia, and racism. These debates demonstrate among other things that Muslims and non-Muslims alike are far from passive in the face of Islamophobia.

In the case of a controversial *Maclean's* magazine article, discussed below, claims about Islamophobia are well grounded; elsewhere, however, the claim seems exaggerated.

Maclean's and Islamophobia

In October 2006 *Maclean's* published an article titled "The New World Order" featuring excerpts from author Mark Steyn's (2006) book *America Alone*. The book was highly critical of Islam and painted an unflattering picture of the dangers posed by Muslim immigrants and their children to Western civilization. The excerpts from Steyn's book focused on the demographic crisis facing many Western societies, including Canada, and how the future of these societies "belonged to Islam." "Everything starts with demography," he claimed, pointing out that Western countries are aging and birthrates are falling. He contrasts this to Muslim societies in the West and in Asia, Africa, and the Middle East, where the birth rate is higher. Growing numbers of Muslims in the West provide what he calls "jihadist" cover for their anti-democratic agenda of terror and chaos. Where native Western populations are aging demographically, they are being "remorselessly" replaced by a young Muslim demographic. Steyn notes that there are "obligatory 'of courses'" to insert, such as "of course" not all Muslims are terrorists; nevertheless, he insists that there are enough Muslims who are "hot for jihad" to create a network of mosques throughout the West.

Though Steyn is careful to say that not all Muslims support terrorism, he thinks that many do share the basic long-term objective of terrorists, which in his view is to impose Islamic law in western democracies. Thus, even if they do not outwardly support terrorist causes, moderate Muslims and their communities in the West nonetheless provide a supportive environment within which "jihad" operates. Steyn contrasts the Irish Republican Army tactics in Northern Ireland in the 1970s and 1980s with "European jihadist" tactics in western Europe today to seemingly differentiate between "good terrorists and bad terrorists." He suggests that "despite the nuttiness of the terrorists' demands," the IRA bombings of public places occurred in defiance of democracy; for "jihadists," on the other hand, terrorist attacks on public places are they way they practice democracy.

Further, in the excerpts of the book reproduced by *Maclean's*, Muslim immigrants are portrayed as a foreign presence in Western societies. Muslims are seen as having no loyalty to their Western countries of residence or citizenship. Their loyalties are primarily to other places, and ideas: "Western Muslim's pan-Islamic identity is merely the first great cause in a world where globalized pathologies are taking place of old school nationalism." As a result, Steyn predicts a future of violence and disorder in the West coming largely from its Muslim population. He also characterized Muslims, particularly youth, as naturally violent, recounting media and government authorities' characterization of the unrest as "youth" violence. According to Steyn, these sources lacked the courage to name the violence for what it really was—"Muslim youth violence."

In Steyn's view, Western governments and many of their well-meaning citizens and institutions are bending over backwards to accommodate Muslims and to avoid insulting Muslim sensibilities.

> How does the state react? In Seville, King Ferdinand III is no longer patron saint of the annual fiesta because his splendid record in fighting for Spanish independence from the Moors was felt to be insensitive to Muslims. In London, a judge agreed to the removal of Jews and Hindus from a trial jury because the Muslim defendant's counsel argued he couldn't get a fair verdict from them. The Church of England is considering removing St. George as the country's patron saint on the grounds that, according to various Anglican clergy, he's too "militaristic" and "offensive to Muslims." They wish to replace him with St. Alban, and replace St. George's cross on the revamped Union Flag, which would instead show St. Alban's cross as a thin yellow streak. (Steyn 2006a)

Steyn argues that governments and institutions are taking these tacks because of a fear of backlash from their respective Muslim communities. He alleges that Western governments live in fear of Muslim violence and are too willing to accommodate themselves to Islam. In his view, radicalized Islamists are experts at exploiting the tolerance of Western societies (Steyn 2006a). "Multiculturalism" is not an ideology that constitutes an effective glue to keep Western societies together. Like other critics of multicultural policy in this country, he suggests that it fosters division, separation, and new forms of fundamentalism.

Maclean's was taken before the British Columbia Human Rights Tribunal in 2008. Mohammad Elmasry, President of the Canadian Islamic Congress, and Naiyer Habib, a cardiologist from Abbotsford, British Columbia, lodged a complaint before the Tribunal. The specific complaint was that the *Maclean's* article exposed Muslims in British Columbia to hatred and contempt, which is contrary to Section 7 of the Human Rights Code of the province. In its judgment, the BC tribunal did recognize that the article contained "historical, religious and factual inaccuracies" and that it "used common Muslim stereotypes" (*Elmasry and Habib v. Rogers Publishing and MacQueen* 2008, 33). The tribunal was reluctant to admit that the article was a form of Islamophobia, though, because the complainants and their witnesses offered no definition of the term. In the end, however, the tribunal rejected the complaint on the grounds that the article was a legitimate contribution to public debate and that while it may have raised fears in reader's minds about Muslims, "fear is not synonymous with hatred and contempt" (*Elmasry and Habib v. Rogers Publishing and MacQueen* 2008, 37).

Allegations that *Maclean's* promotes Islamophobia and fear of Muslims continue. A report prepared by graduates of Osgood Hall Law School argues that a number of articles published by the magazine between 2005 and 2007 "demonstrates that *Maclean's* is engaging in a discriminatory form of journalism that targets the Muslim community, promotes stereotypes, misrepresents fringe elements as the mainstream Muslim community, and distorts facts to present a false image of Muslims" (Awan et al. 2009, 4).

Toronto Life and "honour killing"

In June 2010, Muhammad Parvez and his son Waqas pleaded guilty to the December 2007 murder of 16-year-old Aqsa Parvez, Muhammad's daughter. She was the youngest of eight children of Pakistani immigrants who came to Canada several years earlier. According to reports, Parvez refused to conform to her father's expectations of how a young Muslim girl should behave: she refused to wear the hijab, wore Western clothing, and resisted an arranged marriage with a man in Pakistan. She ran away from home twice in fall 2007. The first time she ran away, she went to a shelter that a school guidance counsellor recommended. The second time, she stayed at a friend's house, and while waiting at a bus stop to go to school, her brother Waqas persuaded her to come home so that she could collect some of her belongings. A few minutes later, Muhammad Parvez called 911 saying he had killed his daughter (Allen and Friesen 2010).

In 2008 before the case went to trail, *Toronto Life* magazine published an article that became yet another touch point for accusations of Islamophobia, racism, and the unfair treatment of Muslims in the media. Much of the controversy surrounded the claim made by author Mary Rogan that Aqsa Parvez was the victim of an "honour killing." The article described how there was debate over Aqsa Parvez's death being murder or domestic violence. Rogan noted that worldwide, some five thousand women die in so-called honour killings, and many of these are in Pakistan (*Toronto Life* 2008).

The article went on to put this apparent honour killing in the wider context of the failure of Canadian multicultural policy and the apparent unwillingness of Muslims to integrate into Canadian society. Although we are proud of our multicultural society and our attitudes toward institutionalized patriarchy, Rogan pointed to debates over sharia law, the Toronto 18, and young girls wearing hijabs at soccer games, and asked if Toronto society has become "too tolerant" of cultural difference.

The story provoked outrage among some readers. They accused both the magazine's publisher and the author of racism. Critics argued that Aqsa Parvez's murder was a form of domestic violence. Feminists stressed that the murder had everything to do with patriarchy, but little to do with Pakistani culture or Islam; to describe the incident as an honour killing unfairly cast Muslim families and child rearing practices more generally, and immigrants from Pakistan in particular, in a negative light. As such, it was racist. Michelle Cho, of the Urban Alliance on Race Relations, was one of the harshest critics to respond to the article.

Defining Parvez's murder as an honour killing may be an instance of racialization, but it is not obvious that it qualifies as racism. It is a form of racialization because it attaches significance to culture, religion, and indirectly race as the interpretation of domestic violence. However, Cho's and others' reactions to the article may be a case where the term racism is used too broadly and as a form of political abuse. The *Toronto Life* piece does characterize Canadian multicultural policy in a negative light, but that does not make it racist. However, is the claim that "Muslims are not integrating" racist? This is a widespread perception in Canada, and elsewhere,

Toronto Life Faces Criticism for Aqsa Parvez Story

11 November 2008

Ms. Rogan and Ms. Fulford,

When I read this article, I was outraged. While I'm glad that Aqsa has not been forgotten, I am dismayed by the way she is being remembered and how her death has been sensationalized to further an anti-immigration, Islamophobic and racist rhetoric. This is irresponsible journalism and only polarizes the issues and our communities. This article feeds into fear mongering—an Us vs. Them mentality by suggesting that embracing diversity is a runaway train leading to the death of liberalism as we know it. The suggestion that Aqsa's murder is an indication that multiculturalism has "gone too far" is offensive and assumes that this gender violence is linked to one's culture and religion—rather than an individual's criminal behaviour supported by a society that refuses to acknowledge the larger context of violence against women.

When Robert Picton was convicted of murdering 26 Vancouver sex trade workers, his criminality was not linked to his Whiteness or being a farmer for that matter. Nor has the recent and tragic murder of Susan Ryan by her police officer husband lead to the assumption that all police are murderers. How is it that the abusive behaviour of the one man legitimizes Ms. Rogan to put a whole religious community on trial, in violation of "our" liberal values? Whose values are we talking about here? The implications are that "West is Best", that all Muslims should be adapting to "our" way of life, ignoring the fact that we are all immigrants to this country living on stolen land.

Communities of colour should not be absolved from acknowledging the ways in which they perpetuate gender violence. However, institutional changes need to be made to challenge the systemic racism that is embedded in our legal system and create supports so that women of colour can feel safe to report acts of sexual violence. But gender violence is not just an issue facing women of colour. The fact is that 51% of women in Canada have experienced at least one incidence of physical or sexual violence since the age of 16. Bottom line: Violence against women affects ALL women regardless of where you're from.

You have the power to shape public thinking on an issue and influence public policy. To point to the imagined incendiary nature of what is a peaceful religion is to take attention away from the fact that a young woman was killed. What needs to be addressed is the crisis of gender violence in this country and the kind of racist thinking that only serves to exacerbate the divisions in our communities. I would encourage [that] Toronto Life seriously examine [its] commitment to civic journalism, in ways that support dialogue. Providing opportunities for your journalists and editors to examine their racial bias, Islamophobia and sexism would help to provide a thoughtful and balanced coverage that can feature the real Toronto.

Respectfully,

Michelle Cho
Urban Alliance on Race Relations

Source: *Toronto Life* 2008

but it is probably exaggerated, as is Muslims' lack of commitment to Canada. A 2007 Environics poll showed, for example, that despite their concerns about unemployment and immigration-related issues, many Muslims are integrating into Canadian society. The vast majority report being "very proud" to be Canadian (CBC 2007). However, mistaken ideas about Muslim integration are not necessarily racist.

By the time that Aqsa Parvez's father and brother admitted the murder in 2010, the notion of an honour killing was less controversial. The leader of the Muslim Canadian Congress is reported to have said that "the guilty plea is a wake-up call for parents to understand that young women are not the possessions of men. Muslim leaders who do not call Ms. Parvez's murder and honour killing are avoiding the real issue" (Allen and Friesen 2010, A8).

There are many other instances where Muslims and Islam have been portrayed in Canadian media and around the world in an unflattering light. The popular CBC program *Little Mosque on the Prairie*, which is a lighthearted comedy focusing on the ordinary relationships between Muslims and non-Muslims in a fictional prairie town, is an important exception. Although, even that program generates suspicion in some Canadian's minds—one commentator in a *Globe and Mail* online chat with the show's creator, Zarqa Nawaz, thought that the show was a cover for al Quaeda (*Globe and Mail* 2007)! More significantly, though, the reporting of the case of the Toronto 18 and the Danish cartoon affair both generated considerable controversy about media reporting of issues involving Islam and Muslims. Concerns have been raised about whether the media coverage used Islamophobic, racist, and unflattering stereotypes of fanatical Muslims to interpret these and other events. In many ways, the debate about Islamophobia is parallel to the wider debate about racism raised earlier (see pp. 4–5). Does any reference to Islam or Muslims necessarily mean that an individual or organization is Islamophobic? The answer is no: labelling any reference to Islam or to Muslims as Islamophobic or racist (or both) may obscure more than it reveals. In both cases, the test of racism and/or Islamophobia requires more stringency; it must consider the extent to which difference, whether it is physical, cultural, and/or religious, is constructed as fixed and unchanging, and is negatively evaluated. Certainly, much of the coverage of Muslims in the West is undoubtedly Islamophobic and racist, but this claim requires careful unpacking and attention to nuance and context.

Chapter 7

Solutions for Change

Imp

In 2007 Leger Marketing and Sun Media conducted an online survey on racial tolerance in Canada. One of the survey questions was, "Personally, to what extent do you consider yourself as someone who is racist?" The survey found that just over half of respondents reported being "not at all racist." Forty-seven percent reported to be racist to some extent: one percent "strongly racist," eight percent "moderately racist," and another 38 percent "slightly racist" (Sun Media 2007).

What are we to make of a finding that suggests that nearly half of Canadians admit to being at least "slightly racist"? If we take the findings at face value, it seems to be a disturbing insight into a country that prides itself on tolerance and support for equality and human rights. However, like most, this survey raises more questions than it answers. Are the people who responded to the online poll really representative of Canadians as a whole? Or were these respondents more likely than other Canadians to have negative feelings about other groups and keen to express those feelings? Does the poll mean that nearly half of Canadians see others as biologically inferior or does it reflect occasional negative feelings? Alternatively, some people might think that noticing points of human variation, like skin colour, is racism. Is the willingness to admit to holding racist views a sign that Canadians are finally coming to terms with certain truths about ourselves? Another possibility: given that the allegation of racism is used so often in public debate, do these results reflect a trivialization of the issue?

My own view is that the findings probably represent an inflated estimate of racism in Canada. Looking back over the past 70 years, this country has undergone remarkable transformations in its attitude toward racialized groups. These changes in attitude are reflected in public policy and institutional arrangements. When Canada entered World War II, Chinese Canadians and Aboriginal peoples could not vote in federal elections, or in elections in most provinces. Today, Chinese Canadians, Indo-Canadians, black Canadians, and Aboriginal peoples occupy seats in provincial and federal legislatures and other decision-making bodies: Michaëlle Jean, our previous Governor General, came to Canada from Haiti in 1968. Seventy years ago, racialized minorities were at the bottom of the socio-economic ladder. Today, one of Canada's richest men is an immigrant from Jamaica: entrepreneur Michael Lee-Chin was born in Jamaica to black and Chinese parents and came to Canada as a young man, becoming successful as an investment fund manager. Seventy years ago the law prohibited Chinese Canadians from taking up the professions of law and pharmacy, and quotas were placed on the number of Jews admitted to McGill University. Today, the person checking your eyesight or performing surgery on you may be white, but that person could equally be of Asian or African heritage. As little as 60 years ago, the most exotic meal you could find in major cities or small towns in Canada was Chinese food at one of the handful of restaurants that had sprung up in the 1920s and 1930s. Today's Toronto is home to over three hundred Italian restaurants; one hundred Chinese and Indian restaurants; and dozens of African, South Asian, Thai, Vietnamese, Japanese, and Caribbean restaurants, among others. A similar pattern is true in other Canadian cities. You might dismiss the availability of a variety of ethnic foods as a simplistic measure of diversity. However, taken in the context of other social changes, it suggests that Canada is undoubtedly a more open, tolerant, and welcoming place than it has been in the past.

Yet statistical survey and personal experience show that racism continues to be a problem in our society. Some see it as a minor problem; others feel it is a much deeper and more significant social issue. As I have suggested in this book, racism is without doubt a real-lived experience for individuals, families, and communities, and remains a pressing social issue in Canadian today. It may not be as significant and widespread as has been in the past, in part because sometimes processes of racialization are mistaken for racism. At the same time, racism persists despite many improvements in the treatment of immigrants, racialized communities, and Aboriginal peoples in this country over the past 70 years.

Multicultural and Anti-racist Education

Education, broadly defined, has probably been the most successful solution to racism and discrimination. There is a long history of education dating back at least to the post–World War II UNESCO conferences (see pp. 6–7). Many scientists, horrified by the atrocities committed in the name of race during the war, embarked on a campaign of education. As we saw above, theories about race were discredited and research findings were made as public as possible.

More recent educational campaigns and initiatives that attempt to address the problem of racism involve cross-cultural sensitivity training and/or anti-racist education. Inspired by multiculturalism, sensitivity training is often directed at people in positions of power, providing education about cultures, values, and religions of other groups of people.

There are numerous examples. Many schools in Canada have cross-cultural food or song-and-dance days that introduce teachers and students to other ethnicities. Organizations like immigrant-aid associations operate host programs that match newcomer families with Canadian families. While their aim is not specifically to combat racism, they do successfully teach immigrants aspects of Canadian culture and help them integrate into Canadian society. They also help newcomers build networks among settled Canadians; this often helps in finding employment. At the same time, Canadian host families learn more about the cultures and backgrounds of new Canadians. Business associations and volunteer groups offer courses and workshops that deal with business and volunteering strategies in cross-cultural settings. And police forces and other organizations sometimes offer seminars and workshops in respectful treatment of diverse ethnicities.

Anti-racist education, on the other hand, seeks to expose issues of power and inequality stemming from difference (Bonnett 2000; Dei 1998). Rather than treating cultural differences as the source of conflict, hostility, and racism, this approach sees racism as the source of conflict and hostility. While there are many forms of anti-racist education, the overall view is to teach majority groups about the power they possess and how their everyday actions, decisions, and assumptions can be discriminatory.

A related approach within anti-racist education is to focus on "white privilege." A university professor presenting to the Canadian Federation of Students-Ontario Task Force on Campus Racism argues that "there is a great need for wider education at all levels on how whiteness reproduces itself in a myriad of subtle and systemic ways. Basic information about white privilege should be taught in first year [university] courses" (Canadian Federation of Students-Ontario 2010, 23).

In the early 1990s, Bob Rae's government began developing an anti-racist program. An Anti-Racism Secretariat was created in part to challenge the shortcomings of the then dominant view in government circles that multiculturalism and cross-cultural education was the solution to rising racial tensions in Toronto. Shortly after the Secretariat was formed in 1991, the NDP government struck a separate commission of inquiry, led by Stephen Lewis, into a series of disturbances in Toronto in the summer of 1992. The disturbances, known as the "Toronto riot," occurred along Yonge Street and followed an anti-racist rally to protest the acquittal of four Los Angeles police officers charged in the beating of black motorist Rodney King (Harney 2002). The Lewis inquiry report was a hard-hitting document that pointed to the shortcomings of intercultural education. It became a strong advocate for a more aggressive anti-racist approach to government policy. According to Lewis:

> What we are dealing with at root, and fundamentally, is anti-black racism. While it is obviously true that every visible minority community experiences indignities and wounds of systemic discrimination throughout Southern Ontario, it is the black community which is the focus. It is blacks who are being shot, it is black youth that [are] unemployed in excessive numbers, it is black students who are inappropriately streamed in schools, it is black kids who are disproportionately dropping out. ... Just as the soothing balm of "multiculturalism" cannot mask racism, so racism cannot mask its primary target. (Lewis 1992)

The Anti-Racism Secretariat did not outlive the NDP government. One of the first official acts of the Conservative government, upon coming to power in 1995, was to dismantle the Secretariat, as well as the wider employment equity initiatives that the NDP had started. But despite this setback, anti-racism initiatives remain a popular solution to ethnic and racial tensions.

While these approaches are clearly well intentioned, one problem is the assumption that racism stems from a lack of knowledge:

White Privilege

In 1988, Peggy McIntosh, a Women's Studies Professor at Wellesley College in Massachusetts, published what became a landmark article about white privilege. McIntosh likens this to an invisible backpack that provides many advantages in social settings. The advantages listed by McIntosh include:

When I am told about our national heritage or about "civilization," I am shown that people of my color made it what it is.

...

I can talk with my mouth full and not have people put this down to my color.

I can swear, or dress in second hand clothes, or not answer letters, without having people attribute these choices to the bad morals, the poverty or the illiteracy of my race.

I can do well in a challenging situation without being called a credit to my race.

I am never asked to speak for all the people of my racial group.

...

If I declare there is a racial issue at hand, or there isn't a racial issue at hand, my race will lend me more credibility for either position than a person of color will have.

...

I can worry about racism without being seen as self-interested or self-seeking.

Source: McIntosh 1988

if only the right information is made available, racism will eventually disappear. Another problem is that some anti-racism education programs end up generating a backlash, making those in power take a defensive stance. Educational initiatives such as these may meet with resistance as few people are willing to cede power and privilege. Further, not everyone accepts that white people are universally privileged and that people of colour are universally disadvantaged. Privilege in Canada is not limited to one set of factors; it also emerges from social class and gender. Clearly, not all white people have access to the corridors of power—many work in minimum wage jobs, are unemployed, or are on social assistance. And, as we noted already, some people of colour have achieved economic success in professions and in the business world. First-generation immigrants and members of racialized communities are making their way into municipal politics, provincial legislatures, and the federal House of Commons (Bloemraad 2006).

While there are limits, education is clearly an important part of the solution. We saw above that racism can arise not from a lack of contact or awareness, but because competition and conflict over limited resources. While there are limits, education is clearly an important part of the solution for those who lack contact with diverse communities and who lack awareness of the problem. As we will see, some other roots of the problem—such as competition and conflict over limited resources—are better resolved with formal regulation.

Is Legislation the Answer?

Michael Banton (2002) argues that focusing on education misdirects time and resources. Education rarely works, he insists, and changing behaviour is easier than changing minds. More effective is to outlaw discriminatory treatment. It may be impossible to change what people *think*, but we can legally prevent acts of injustice through the implementation and enforcement of strong anti-discrimination measures. We can create legal measures to prevent people with racist attitudes from denying jobs, housing, or other opportunities or resources to peoples of colour.

Canada is committed to outlawing discrimination. Federal and provincial human rights legislation protects individuals from discriminatory treatment based on race as well as "national or ethnic origin, colour, religion, age, sex, sexual orientation, marital status, family status, disability or conviction for an offence for which a pardon has been granted" (*Canadian Human Rights Act*). At the federal level, the Canadian Human Rights Commission deals with federal departments, agencies and Crown corporations, chartered banks, airlines, television and radio stations, inter-provincial communication and telephone companies, buses and railways that travel between provinces, and the governing bodies of Aboriginal peoples. Provincial and territorial human rights commissions deal with complaints related to retail and hospitality businesses (stores, restaurants, and hotels), hospitals or health care providers, schools, colleges and universities, and most manufacturers.

The Canadian Human Rights Commission tries to be proactive by working with employers to prevent disputes. When complaints are made, the Commission encourages parties to resolve the grievance informally, or through mediation. As a last resort it can recommend a case be heard before the Canadian Human Rights Tribunal. Such complaints-driven processes are slow-moving and time consuming, and it requires significant effort and resources to bring a case before a Human Rights Tribunal, let alone win.

As some critics have pointed out, human rights tribunals are an imperfect solution to racism and discrimination. They tend to be driven by individual-level complaints, and the remedies are mainly individual (see p. 108). These bodies also have a harder time dealing with issues of systemic or institutional racism where more than one individual is disadvantaged by a particular organizational policy or practice.

Employment equity policy has been another public policy response to racism and discrimination. In Canada it is sometimes mistakenly referred to by the American term "affirmative action." The Federal Employment Equity Act was passed into law in 1986 in order to

achieve equality in the workplace so that no person shall be denied employment opportunities or benefits for reasons unrelated to
ability and, in the fulfillment of the goals, to correct the conditions
of disadvantage in employment experienced by women, Aboriginal
peoples, persons with disabilities, and visible minority people by
giving effect to the principle that employment equity means more
than treating persons in the same way but also requires special

Canadian Human Rights Commission, Settlement Examples, 2009

The Canadian Human Rights Commission publishes a yearly list of settlement examples from cases it deals with. The following are three examples of cases and settlements arrived at in 2009.

Ground(s): National or ethnic origin, religion, sex
Area: Employment
Sector: Transportation
Allegation: The complainant alleged that his supervisor harassed him by making sexual comments regarding the complainant having intercourse with his wife and made sexual gestures with his food. Furthermore, his supervisor asked him if he was part of the Taliban or a terrorist network. The complainant informed the employer of these actions and his employment was subsequently terminated.
Settlement: Financial compensation for damages.

Ground(s): Race
Area: Employment
Sector: Banking
Allegation: The complainant, who is black, alleged that his supervisors harassed him and that his co-workers engaged in racist comments and name-calling. He said he was not only given more work than his colleagues but also paid less. His employment was eventually terminated.
Settlement: Financial compensation for general damages and for legal costs.
Financial compensation for severance and loss of income.

Ground(s): Race, colour, national or ethnic origin
Area: Provision of services
Sector: Communication
Allegation: The complainant, who is a member of a visible minority, alleged that he was treated differently by a representative of his cable provider. The representative harassed him and made racially derogatory comments. The complainant also alleged that when he tried to address the matter, one of the managers treated him in a rude and abusive manner.
Settlement: Free equipment to the complainant and free cable service for one year.

Source: Canadian Human Rights Commission 2009

measures and the accommodation of differences. (Canadian Human Rights Commission 2009)

Like the Canadian Human Rights Commission, employment equity legislation targets federally regulated employers. It also includes organizations with one hundred or more employees who have federal goods or services contracts worth more than $200,000. (This is why, incidentally, universities come under the Federal Employment Equity Act, but under provincial Human Rights codes.) Some federally regulated employers have undertaken considerable effort to diversify their workplaces in line with stated objectives of employment equity policy. Many banks have also been at the forefront of diversifying their workforces, not just because it is good in itself, but also because a more diverse workforce is good for business. On the other hand, some public institutions, where the profit motive is less of an incentive, seem to be lagging behind. In its 2010 report on employment equity in the Federal Public Service, the Standing Senate Committee on Human Rights (2010) suggested that the federal government, as the largest employer in Canada, continues to face challenges in creating a workforce that is truly representative of all Canadians. The Senate Committee pointed out that while women, Aboriginal peoples, and people with disabilities are adequately represented in the ranks of the public service, representation of other people of colour continues to lag behind. It further noted that the four designated groups were under-represented at the upper echelons of the federal public service, that women tended to hold lower-paying jobs than men, and that Aboriginal peoples in the federal public service were not equitably distributed throughout the public service (Senate Standing Committee on Human Rights 2010).

While some far-thinking employers have realized that they can profit from diversifying their workforce, it is equally true that there are certain weaknesses to Canada's approach to employment equity. First, it only covers federally regulated employers, which comprises only some 10 percent of Canada's eighteen-million-strong labour force. Another weakness is that the enforcement mechanisms are limited. To comply with the legislation, federally regulated employers must develop employment equity plans. That is, they must develop plans and strategies to improve employment opportunities for the four designated groups. However, there is nothing in the legislation that forces employers to take any actual action. Instead, the legislation identifies public opinion as the main enforcement mechanism. That is, negative public opinion about laggard employers is expected to encourage/force employers to take action. Bad publicity might motivate organizations to hire individuals of diverse backgrounds, but equally, it may not.

Banton may also underemphasize the significance of education in this process of dealing with racism. For a society to begin implementing proactive measures to eliminate discrimination, it must first be open to such initiatives. People do not naturally and inevitably conclude that their society requires anti-discrimination policies; education can help societies move along to implement the kinds of initiatives Banton advocates.

However, I think any solution to racism needs to begin from an insightful observation made by British sociologist Stuart Hall over 30 years ago. Hall argued that racist attitudes are

> not a set of false pleas which swim around in the head. They're not a set of mistaken perceptions. They have their basis in real material conditions of existence. They arise because of the concrete problems of different classes and groups in society. Racism represents the attempt ideologically to construct those conditions, contradictions and problems in such a way that they can be dealt with and deflected at the same moment. (Hall 1978, 35)

In other words, processes of racialization and the ideology of racism arise out of the sum total of people's values, ideals, and experiences. They come from socialization and interaction with others, but also from contexts where individuals and groups compete for scarce resources. Racialized understandings of how humans differ from one another and racist attitudes and practices are part of the way that some people make sense of, and deal with, the complex world around them. Racism must be documented, condemned, and taken very seriously. However, part of taking racism seriously also involves recognizing that simply labelling an individual, attitude, or practice as racist does not help us explain or understand that racism. It also involves attention to our use of the term and to how particular social conditions lead individuals to both think about race and to evaluate racialized individuals and groups in negative ways.

A Look to the Future

What does the future hold for Canada? Statistics Canada predicts that by 2017, one in five Canadians will be a "visible minority." It is expected that people of colour will make up 50 percent of the population of Toronto and Vancouver, nearly 30 percent of the population of Ottawa, and nearly 25 percent of the population of Calgary and Windsor (Bélanger and Malenfant 2005). Added to this mix is the prediction that religious diversity in Canada is also about to change. Over the next few years, the fastest growing religious affiliations in Canada are expected to be Islam, Hinduism, and Buddhism (Policy Research Initiative 2009). According to the federal government's Policy Research Initiative (2009), this increasing religious diversity is likely to be one of the new "pressure points" that governments, the media, and the wider society will have to face in the future.

Some Canadians regard these interrelated developments with alarm; others are excited by the possibilities that they hold for the development of new ways that Canadians will have to understand themselves as a nation. I cannot, of course, predict how the future of our country will unfold, whether these developments will create more, and different, tensions, or whether we will continue to live and work together. But on the whole, I am more optimistic than pessimistic. Where does my optimism come from?

First, it is important to recognize that the "normal" state of a society is not the absence of tension and conflict. Societies are not normally in a harmonious condition, with tensions only arising as a result of exceptional events. Conflicts and tensions are inevitable in any society. There will always be differences of opinion over issues like poverty, racism, discrimination, let alone same-sex marriage, prostitution, gun control, and climate change (and why the Toronto Maple Leafs can't seem to win the Stanley Cup). While we may achieve "consensus" on some of these issues, most likely we cannot resolve every issue, and it is unreasonable to think that perfect consensus is the norm. Some public debates become settled through the development of laws and legislation, but not everyone necessarily buys into the legislation or law. Some people abide by certain laws but continue to grumble about them, some people break the law, and others go about trying to change the laws. We should not be alarmed over the fact that we have debates and controversies over issues like racism, discrimination, and Islamophobia. New tensions will no doubt arise, but the fact that we can have these debates without them breaking out into violence is a positive sign.

Second, Canada has gone through debates about ethnic, racial, and religious diversity before, and has survived both the debates and the diversity. As we saw above, one hundred years ago social and political elites were very nervous about what the presence of immigrants from China, India, and Southern and Eastern Europe meant for the long-term future of the country. To some, members of these groups seemed exotic because they brought different tastes, clothing styles, and religious beliefs. To others, they seemed too different from the mainstream, and there was a fear of too much diversity. In other cases, the worry was about the labour market and loss of jobs, lowering wages, or undermining the general standard of living. Yet, despite these conflicts, the immigrants who came to Canada one hundred years ago did become Canadian. Even though they may still have attachments to the ethnic and racial identities of their ancestors, and even connections to their ancestral homelands, they nonetheless are indistinguishable from other Canadians on the level of attitudes and values. Canada is a better place for having welcomed these groups.

Third, and related to the above, is that many of the problems of racism and discrimination are experienced more acutely by the first generation of immigrants. This is not to say that the children and grandchildren of immigrants do not face discrimination and racism, but the nature of that racism is different. So is their ability to address it. Further, despite racism and discrimination, the descendants of immigrants do "assimilate." Assimilation sometimes seems like a bad word because it evokes images of a government forcibly trying to change behaviour—recall here our discussion above of residential schools. However, assimilation as a long-term process, involving changes to both the cultures of immigrants and the culture of the host society, does happen even in the absence of government policies of assimilation. It also happens despite the fact that we live in a society that values multiculturalism. Mutual cultural change takes place in schools and at work, in shopping malls, on sports teams, and on the street. Even though the image of the non-assimilating immigrant remains popular in the consciousness of at least some Canadians, it is clear that immigrants and their children change as a result of living in this country, and this country changes as a result of their presence. I am not at all convinced that because a greater proportion of our population will be made up of peoples of colour this process of assimilation will stop, or slow down.

Fourth, a growing population of peoples of colour does not necessarily lead to increased social tension. If diversity is measured by skin tone alone, then Canada will undoubtedly become more diverse. But simply looking at one point of human variation is far too simplistic; "not white" hardly leads to a rise in Canadian diversity. This kind of simplistic equation recalls assumptions that there is a fixed link between skin colour and behaviour. But of course this is not true. It is not obvious that because a person has a darker skin tone that they are inherently different in terms of what they eat, how they spend their leisure time, how they pray, or what they want their children to become. In short, we should stop inferring that "diversity" increases simply from the presence of more people of colour in Canada.

Fifth, Canadians should not think that we are the only country that is struggling with its sense of identity. There are jokes that all we have in common as a nation are hockey, beer, and donuts. To some, these jokes are frustrating; these superficial markers cannot be a basis for our identity and for constituting ourselves as a national community. But other countries have similar trouble defining themselves and determining the actual attributes that make them who they are. In late 2009 and early 2010, the government of France initiated a nation-wide debate around the question "What does it mean to be French today?" The debate asked people in France to consider questions like, "Does the world envy our culinary art?" and "Is France defined by its patrimony, its culture, its language or our churches and cathedrals?" The debate provided the opportunity for anti-immigrant and anti-Muslim sentiments to be expressed publicly. But it was also clear that by the end of the debate, French people expressed considerable ambivalence and uncertainty over what defined them as "French." After over three hundred town-hall-type meetings across France, the best that the government could come up with as an answer to its original question was to ask schools to fly the French flag and to post the 1789 Declaration of the Rights of Man and of the Citizen on the wall in every classroom in the country. Rather than sculpting a grand statement of "Frenchness," the government quietly let the matter drop. National identities are always difficult to define and operationalize; they are made and remade in the context of changing circumstances. The fact that there does not appear to be a fixed "Canadian" identity should not come as any surprise.

And finally, though Canada's policy of multiculturalism is much maligned these days, let us keep in mind that as an ideology, multiculturalism does allow us to discuss and debate identity, cultural practices, our institutions, the police, and the immigration system. It opens up a space for us to negotiate the differences between us that do exist, and to come up with reasonable accommodations. Multiculturalism provides groups of people who are otherwise marginalized by racism and discrimination the opportunity to articulate their concerns, and to hold other Canadians and governments accountable for their actions and for their commitment to diversity.

Further Reading

Chapter 1

Agnew, V. ed. 2007. *Interrogating Race and Racism*. Toronto: University of Toronto Press.

Fleras, A. 2006. *Unequal Relations: An Introduction to Race and Ethnic Dynamics in Canada*, 5th ed. Toronto: Pearson Education Canada.

Hier, S., and B.S. Bolaria. 2007. *Race and Racism in 21st-Century Canada: Continuity, Complexity, and Change*. Toronto: University of Toronto Press.

Hill Collins, P., and J. Solomos, eds. 2010. *The SAGE Handbook of Race and Ethnic Studies*. London: Sage Publications.

Montagu, A. 1972. *Statement on Race: Annotated Elaboration and Exposition of the Four Statements on Race Issued by Unesco*. Oxford: Oxford University Press.

Chapter 2

Banton, M. 1987. *Racial Theories*. London: Cambridge University Press.

James, C. 2005. *Race in Play: Understanding the Socio-Cultural World of Student Athletes*. Toronto: Canadian Scholars' Press.

Miles, R. 1982. *Racism and Migrant Labour*. London: Routledge & Kegan Paul.

Rex, J., and D. Mason, eds. 1986. *Theories of Race and Ethnic Relations*. Cambridge: Cambridge University Press.

van den Berghe, P. 1986. Ethnicity and the Sociobiology Debate. In *Theories of Race and Ethnic Relations*, eds. J. Rex and D. Mason. Cambridge: Cambridge University Press.

Chapter 3

Abu-Laban, Y., and C. Gabriel. 2008. *Selling Diversity: Immigration, Multiculturalism, Employment Equity, and Globalization*. Toronto: University of Toronto Press.

Avery, D.H. 1995. *Reluctant Host: Canada's Response to Immigrant Workers, 1896–1994*. Toronto: McClelland & Stewart.

Iacovetta, F. 2006. *Gatekeepers: Reshaping Immigrant Lives in Cold War Canada*. Toronto: Between the Lines Press.

Madibbo, A. 2006. *Minority within a Minority: Black Francophone Immigrants and the Dynamics of Power and Resistance*. New York: Routledge.

Mitchell, K. 2004. *Crossing the Neoliberal Line: Pacific Rim Migration and the Metropolis*. Philadelphia: Temple University Press.

Chapter 4

Adams, H. 1999. *Tortured People: The Politics of Colonization*. Penticton: Theytus Books.

Monture-Angus, P. 1995. *Thunder in My Soul: A Mohawk Woman Speaks*. Halifax: Fernwood Publishing.

Pettipas, K. 1994. *Severing the Ties that Bind: Government Repression of Indigenous Religious Ceremonies on the Prairies*. Winnipeg: University of Manitoba Press.

Schissel, B., and T. Wotherspoon. 2002. *The Legacy of School for Aboriginal People: Education, Oppression, and Emancipation*. Toronto: Oxford University Press.

Titley, E.B. 1986. *A Narrow Vision: Duncan Campbell Scott and the Administration of Indian Affairs in Canada*. Vancouver: University of British Columbia Press.

Voyageur, C. 2008. *Firekeepers of the Twenty-First Century: First Nations Women Chiefs*. Montreal and Kingston: McGill-Queen's University Press.

Chapter 5

Mosher, C.J. 1998. *Discrimination and Denial: Systemic Racism in Ontario's Legal and Criminal Justice Systems, 1892–1961*. Toronto: University of Toronto Press.

Royal Commission on Aboriginal Peoples. 1996. *Bridging the Cultural Divide: A Report on Aboriginal People and Criminal Justice in Canada*. Ottawa: Supply and Services Canada.

Tanovich, D. 2005. *The Colour of Justice: Policing Race in Canada*. Toronto: Irwin Law.

Tator, C., and F. Henry. 2006. *Racial Profiling in Canada: Challenging the Myth of a 'Few Bad Apples.'* Toronto: University of Toronto Press.

Wortley, S., and J. Tanner. 2003. Data, Denials and Confusion: The Racial Profiling Debate in Toronto. *Canadian Journal of Criminology and Criminal Justice* 45 (3): 1–9.

Chapter 6

Huntington, S. 1997. *The Clash of Civilizations and the Remaking of the World Order*. New York: Simon & Schuster.

Joppke, C. 2009. *Veil: Mirror of Identity*. Cambridge: Polity Press.

Modood, T., A. Triandafyllidou, and R. Zapata-Barrero, eds. 2006. *Multiculturalism, Muslims and Citizenship: A European Approach*. London: Routledge.

Razack, S. 2008. *Casting Out: The Eviction of Muslims from Western Law and Politics*. Toronto: University of Toronto Press.

Said, F. W. 1978. *Orientalism*. New York: Pantheon.

Chapter 7

Adeyanju, C. 2010. *Deadly Fever: Racism, Disease and a Media Panic*. Halifax: Fernwood Publishing.

Agnew, V. 1996. *Resisting Discrimination: Women from Asia, Africa, and the Caribbean and the Women's Movement in Canada*. Toronto: University of Toronto Press.

Allahar, A. 1998. Race and Racism: Strategies of Resistance. In *Racism and Social Inequality in Canada: Concepts, Controversies & Strategies of Resistance*, ed. V. Satzewich. Toronto: Thompson Educational Publishers.

Bonnett, A. 1993. *Radicalism, Anti-Racism and Representation*. London: Routledge.

Henry, F., and C. Tator, eds. 2009. *Racism in the Canadian University: Demanding Social Justice, Inclusion, and Equity*. Toronto: University of Toronto Press.

Quebec. 2008. Consultation Commission on Accommodation Practices Related to Cultural Differences. *Building the Future: A Time for Reconciliation*. By G. Bouchard and C. Taylor. Available online.

References

Abella, I., and H. Troper. 1982. *None Is Too Many: Canada and the Jews of Europe, 1933–1948*. Toronto: Lester & Orpen Dennys.

Aboriginal Healing Foundation. 2003. Mental Health Profiles for a Sample of British Columbia's Aboriginal Survivors of the Canadian Residential School System. Ottawa: Aboriginal Healing Foundation.

Alberta Federation of Labour. 2009. Entrenching Exploitation: The Second Report of the Alberta Federation of Labour Temporary Foreign Worker Advocate. Edmonton: Alberta Federation of Labour.

Alfred, T. 1995. *Heeding the Voices of Our Ancestors: Kahnawake Mohawk Politics and the Rise of Native Nationalism*. Toronto: Oxford University Press.

———. 1999. *Peace, Power, Righteousness: An Indigenous Manifesto*. Toronto: Oxford University Press.

Allen, K., and J. Friesen. 2010. Father, Brother Plead Guilty to Murder of Daughter. *Globe and Mail*, 15 June: A1, A8.

Amnesty International. 2009. No More Stolen Sisters: The Need for a Comprehensive Response to Discrimination and Violence Against Indigenous Women in Canada. London: Amnesty International.

Amnesty International Canada. 2004. Stolen Sisters: Human Rights Response to Discrimination and Violence Against Women in Canada. Ottawa: Amnesty International Canada.

———. 2005. How Many More Sisters and Daughters Do We Have to Lose? Canada's Continued Failure to Address Discrimination and Violence Against Indigenous Women. Public Brief, 24 October. Ottawa: Amnesty International Canada.

Andersen, K. 1991. *Vancouver's Chinatown: Racial Discourse in Canada, 1875–1980*. Montreal and Kingston: McGill-Queen's University Press.

Anderson, A., and J. Frideres. 1980. *Ethnicity in Canada: Theoretical Perspectives*. Toronto: Butterworths.

Arat-Koc, S. 1992. Immigration Policies, Migrant Domestic Workers and the Definition of Citizenship in Canada. In *Deconstructing a Nation: Immigration, Multiculturalism and Racism in '90s Canada*, ed. V. Satzewich. Halifax: Fernwood Press.

———. 2006. Whose Transnationalism? Canada, "Clash of Civilizations" Discourse, and Arab and Muslim Canadians. In *Transnational Identities and Practices in Canada,* eds. V. Satzewich and L. Wong. Vancouver: University of British Columbia Press.

Association of Black Law Enforcers. 2003. Official Position on "Racial Profiling" in Canada. Toronto: Association of Black Law Enforcers.

Awan, K., et al. 2009. *Maclean's Magazine: A Case Study of Media-Propagated Islamophobia.* Unpublished manuscript.

Backhouse, C. 1999. *Colour-Coded: A Legal History of Racism in Canada, 1900–1950.* Toronto: University of Toronto Press.

Bahdi, R. 2003. No Exit: Racial Profiling and Canada's War Against Terrorism. *Osgood Hall Law Journal* 41 (2–3): 293–316.

Bakan, A., and D. Stasiulis, eds. 1997. *Not One of the Family: Foreign Domestic Workers in Canada.* Toronto: University of Toronto Press.

Ballis Lal, B. 1995. Symbolic Interaction Theories. *American Behavioral Scientist* 38: 421–41.

Banton, M. 1970. The Concept of Racism. In *Race and Racialism*, ed. S. Zubaida. London: Tavistock.

———. 1977. *The Idea of Race.* London: Tavistock.

———. 1995. Rational Choice Theories. *American Behavioral Scientist* 38: 478–97.

———. 2002. *The International Politics of Race.* Cambridge: Cambridge University Press.

Barkan, E. 1992. *The Retreat of Scientific Racism.* Cambridge: Cambridge University Press.

Barker, M. 1981. *The New Racism.* London: Junction Books.

Basok, T. 2002. *Tortillas and Tomatoes: Transmigrant Mexican Harvesters in Canada.* Montreal and Kingston: McGill-Queen's University Press.

Bélanger, A., and É. Caron Malenfant. 2005. Population Projections of Visible Minority Groups, Canada, Provinces and Regions, 2001 to 2017. Ottawa: Statistics Canada. Catalogue 91–541.

Bissoondath, N. 1994. *Selling Illusions: The Cult of Multiculturalism.* Toronto: Penguin Books.

Bloemraad, I. 2006. *Becoming a Citizen: Incorporating Immigrants and Refugees in Canada and the United States.* Berkeley: University of Cailifornia Press.

Bobo, L., and C. Fox. 2003. Race, Racism, and Discrimination: Bridging Problems Methods, and Theory in Social Psychological Research. *Social Psychological Quarterly* 66 (4): 319–32.

Bogardus, E. 1925. Social Distance and Its Origins. *Journal of Applied Sociology* 9: 216–26.

Bolaria, B.S., and P. Li. 1988. *Racial Oppression in Canada*. 2nd ed. Toronto: Garamond Press.

Bonacich, E. 1972. A Theory of Ethnic Antagonism: The Split Labour Market. *American Sociological Review* 37: 547–59.

———. 1976. Advanced Capitalism and Black-White Relations in the United States: A Split Labour Market Interpretation. *American Sociological Review* 41: 34–51.

———. 1979. The Past, Present and Future of Split Labour Market Theory. In *Research in Race and Ethnic Relations: A Research Annual*, eds. C.B. Marrett and C. Leggon. Vol. 1. 17–64. Greenwich, CT: JAI Press.

———. 1980. Class Approaches to Ethnicity and Race. *Insurgent Sociologist* 10 (2): 9–23.

Bonnett, A. 2000. *Anti-Racism*. London: Routledge.

Bouchard, G., and B.W. Carroll. 2002. Policy-Making and Administrative Discretion: The Case of Immigration in Canada. *Canadian Public Administration* 45 (2): 239–57.

Brand, D., and K. Sri Bhaggiyadatta. 2003. Rivers Have Sources, Trees Have Roots. In *Histories of Canadian Children and Youth*, eds. N. Janovicek and J. Parr. Toronto: Oxford University Press.

Brasfield, C. 2001. The Residential School Syndrome. *BC Medical Journal* 43 (2): 78–81.

Brown, H. 2007. Why I Fired Professor Churchill. *WSJ.com*, 26 July. Available online.

Brown, R. 1995. *Prejudice: Its Social Psychology*. Oxford: Blackwell Publishers.

Brym, R., and R. Lenton. 1993. The Distribution of Anti-Semitism in Canada in 1984. In *The Jews in Canada*, eds. R. Brym, W. Shaffir, and M. Weinfeld. Toronto: Oxford University Press.

Bullock, K., and G.J. Jafri. 2000. Media (Mis)representations: Muslim Women in the Canadian Nation. *Canadian Woman Studies* 20 (2): 35–40.

Calliste, A. 1987. Sleeping Car Porters in Canada: An Ethnically Submerged Split Labour Market. *Canadian Ethnic Studies* 19 (1): 1–20.

———. 1991. Canada's Immigration Policy and Domestics from the Caribbean: The Second Domestic Scheme. In *Race, Class, Gender: Bonds and Barriers*, eds. J. Vorst et al. 136–68. Toronto: Garamond Press.

———. 1996. Antiracism Organizing and Resistance in Nursing: African Canadian Women. *Canadian Review of Sociology and Anthropology* 33 (3): 361–90.

Canada. 1947. House of Commons Debates. Vol. 3. Ottawa.

———. 1991. Multiculturalism and Citizenship. Multiculturalism and Canadians: Attitude Study 1991. Report submitted to Multiculturalism and Citizenship Canada by Angus Reid Group. Ottawa.

———. 2005. Department of Canadian Heritage. Canada's Action Plan Against Racism. Ottawa.

———. 2008. Citizenship and Immigration. Facts and Figures 2007—

Immigration Overview: Permanent and Temporary Residents. Ottawa. Available online.

———. 2009. Canadian Human Rights Commission. Settlement Examples for 2009. Ottawa. Available online.

Canadian Broadcasting Corporation (CBC). 2007. Glad to Be Canadian, Muslims Say. *CBC.ca*, 13 February. Available online.

———. 2008. B.C. Apologizes for Komagata Maru Incident. *CBC.ca*, 23 May. Available online.

———. 2010. Indian Status Coming for Thousands of Canadians. *CBC.ca*, 10 March. Available online.

Canadian Broadcasting Corporation (CBC) Manitoba. 2008. The New Wave: The Immigrant Experience in Manitoba. 28 April to 2 May.

Canadian Council for Refugees. 2010. Safe Third Country, Overview. *CCRweb.ca*. Available online.

Canadian Federation of Students (CFS) Ontario. 2010. The Final Report of the Task Force on Campus Racism. Toronto: CFS-Ontario.

Canadian Human Rights Act, RS 1985, c .H-6.

Canadian Human Rights Commission. 2009. Settlement Examples for 2009. Ottawa: Canadian Human Rights Commission. Available online.

Canadian Press. 2010. Nisga'a Nation Celebrates Historic Treaty Anniversary. *CTV News British Columbia*, 29 June. Available online.

Canadian Race Relations Foundation. 2001. Canada's Immigration Polices: Contradictions and Shortcomings'. *CRRF Perspectives: Focus on Immigration and Refugee Issues* (Autumn/Winter).

Carter, S. 1990. *Lost Harvests: Prairie Indian Reserve Farmers and Government Policy*. Montreal and Kingston: McGill-Queen's University Press.

Castles, S., and G. Kosack. 1973. *Immigrant Workers and Class Structure in Western Europe*. London: Oxford University Press.

Castles, S., and M. Miller. 2003. *The Age of Migration: International Population Movements in the Modern World*. 3rd ed. New York: Guilford.

Chrisjohn, R., and S. Young. 1995. *The Circle Game: Shadow and Substance in the Residential School Experience*. Penticton: Theytus Books.

Churchill, W. 2005. Ward Churchill Statement. *Commondreams.org*, 1 February. Available online.

Collingwood Enterprise-Bulletin. 2009. Area Farmers Fear Swine Flu Impact. *Canoe.ca*, 1 May. Available online.

Coloma, T. 2010. 100,000 Immigrants $100-Billion in Trade. *Globe and Mail*, 15 May: A17.

Commission des droits de la personne et des droits de la jeunesse. 2010. Racial Profiling: Consultation Document on Racial Profiling. Montreal: Commissions des droits de la personne et des droits de la jeunesse.

Commission on British Muslims and Islamophobia. 1997. Islamophobia: A Challenge For Us All. London: The Runnymede Trust.

———. 2004. Islamophobia: Issues, Challenges, Action: A Report by the

Commission on British Muslims and Islamophobia. Stoke-on-Trent: Trentham Books.

Commission on Systemic Racism in the Ontario Criminal Justice System. 1995. Final Report of the Commission on Systemic Racism in the Ontario Criminal Justice System. Toronto: Queen's Printer for Ontario.

Cormier, G. 2007. Defending Churchill. *Nova News Net*. Available online.

Cox, O.C. 1948. *Caste, Class and Race: A Study in Social Dynamics*. New York: Doubleday.

Danys, M. 1986. *DP: Lithuanian Immigration to Canada after the Second World War*. Toronto: Multicultural History Society of Ontario.

Dei, G. 1998. The Politics of Educational Change: Taking Anti-Racism Education Seriously. In *Racism and Social Inequality in Canada*, ed. V. Satzewich. Toronto: Thomson Educational Publishers.

Deputy Minister of Citizenship and Immigration. 1964. Memorandum. National Archives of Canada. RG26. Volume 124. File 3-33-6. Part 2.

Director of Immigration to Deputy Minister of Immigration. 1955. Memorandum. National Archives of Canada. RG26. Volume 124. File 3-33-6. Part 1.

Doob, C. 1996. *Racism: An American Cauldron*. New York: HarperCollins.

Dunk, T. 1991. *It's a Working Man's Town: Male Working-Class Culture*. Montreal and Kingston: McGill-Queen's University Press.

Dyck, N. 1991. *What is the Indian "Problem": Tutelage and Resistance in Canadian Indian Administration*. St. John's: Institute of Social and Economic Research.

Edwards, B.F.R. 2005. *Paper Talk: A History of Libraries, Print Culture, and Aboriginal Peoples in Canada before 1960*. Lanham, MD: Scarecrow Press.

EKOS Research Associates. 2006. *Perceptions of First Nations Residents On-Reserve: Study Results*. Ottawa: EKOS Research Associates.

———. 2007. *Canada Border Services Agency: Baseline Study*. Ottawa: EKOS Research Associates.

Elmasry and Habib v. Rogers Publishing and MacQueen. 2008. British Columbia Human Rights Tribunal (4): 378.

Feagin, J., and H. Vera. 1995. *White Racism: The Basics*. New York: Routledge.

Feagin, J., H. Vera, and P. Batur. 2001. *White Racism: The Basics*. 2nd ed. New York: Routledge.

Flanagan, T. 2000. *First Nations, Second Thoughts*. Kingston and Montreal: McGill-Queen's University Press.

Frideres, J., and R. Gadacz. 2008. *Aboriginal Peoples in Canada*. 8th ed. Toronto: Pearson Education Canada.

Friesen, J. 2005. Another Funeral, This One Well-Guarded. *Globe and Mail*, 28 November: A11.

Fulford, R. 2006. How We Became a Land of Ghettos. *The National Post*, 12 June: A19.

Furi, M., and J. Wherrett. 2003. Indian Status and Band Membership Issues. Ottawa: Parliamentary Research Branch, Library of Parliament.

Galabuzi, G.-E. 2006. *Canada's Economic Apartheid: The Social Exclusion of Racialized Groups in the New Century*. Toronto: Canadian Scholars Press.

Garner, S. 2010. *Racisms: An Introduction*. Los Angeles: Sage.

Globe and Mail. 2007. Little Mosque on the Prairie. *Globeandmail.com*, 9 January. Available online.

Goutor, D. 2007. *Guarding the Gates: The Canadian Labour Movement and Immigration, 1872–1934*. Vancouver: University of British Columbia Press.

Gova, A., and R. Kurd. 2008. *The Impact of Racial Profiling*. Working Paper 08–14. Vancouver: Metropolis British Columbia.

Greenaway, N. 2010. Education Pays Off for Canada's Aboriginal Women: Study. Canwest News Service, April 8. Available online.

Hall, S. 1978. Racism and Reaction. In *Commission for Racial Equality, Five Views of Multi-Racial Britain*. London: Commission for Racial Equality.

Hamdan, A. 2009. *Muslim Women Speak: A Tapestry of Lives and Dreams*. Toronto: Women's Press.

Harney, S. 2002. *State Work: Public Administration and Mass Intellectuality*. Durham, NC: Duke University Press.

Harvey, E.B. 2003. An Independent Review of the Toronto Star Analysis of Criminal Information Processing System (CIPS) Data Provided by the Toronto Police Services (TPS): A Summary Report. Toronto: Toronto Police Service.

Hechter, M. 1995. Explaining Nationalist Violence. *Nations and Nationalism* 1 (1): 53–86.

Henry, F., and E. Ginzberg. 1985. *Who Gets the Work? A Test of Racial Discrimination in Employment*. Toronto: Urban Alliance on Race Relations and the Social Planning Council of Metropolitan Toronto.

Henry, F., and C. Tator. 2010. *The Colour of Democracy: Racism in Canada*. 4th ed. Toronto: Thomson Nelson.

Henry, M., and T. Huffman. 2006. Dead, Innocent, Black, White. *Toronto Star*, 17 October: B4.

Herrnstein, R., and C. Murray. 1994. *The Bell Curve: Intelligence and Class Structure in American Life*. New York: Free Press.

Hitchens, C. 2009. Assassins of the Mind. *Vanity Fair*, February. Available online.

Hum, D., and W. Simpson. 2007. Revisiting Equity and Labour: Immigration, Gender, Minority Status, and Income in Canada. In *Race and Racism in 21ˢᵗ Century Canada: Continuity, Complexity, and Change*, eds. S. Hier and S. Bolaria. 89–109. Peterborough: Broadview Press.

Huntington, S. 2006. Five Years After 9/11, the Clash of Civilizations Revisited—Interview. *The Pew Forum on Religion and Public Life*. 18 August. Available online.

Iacovetta, F. 1992. *Such Hardworking People: Italian Immigrants in Post-War Toronto*. Toronto: University of Toronto Press.

——. 2006. *Gatekeepers: Reshaping Immigrant Lives in Cold War Canada*. Toronto: Between the Lines Press.

Islamophobia Watch: Documenting Anti-Muslim Bigotry. n.d. About Us. Available online.

Jakubowski, L. 1997. *Immigration and the Legalization of Racism*. Halifax: Fernwood Press.

Johnson, H. 1989. *The Voyage of the Komagata Maru*. Vancouver: University of British Columbia Press.

Johnson, J., W. Farrel, and C. Guinn. 1999. Immigration Reform and the Browning of America: Tensions, Conflicts and Community Instability in Metropolitan Los Angeles. In *The Handbook of International Migration: The American Experience*, eds. C. Hirschman et al. New York: Russell Sage Foundation.

Joppke, C. 2009. *Veil: Mirror of Identity*. Cambridge: Polity Press.

Kallen, E. 2003. *Ethnicity and Human Rights in Canada*. 3rd ed. Toronto: Oxford University Press.

Karim, K. 2009. Changing Perceptions of Islamic Authority among Muslims in Canada, the United States and the United Kingdom. Montreal: Institute for Research on Public Policy.

Kay, J. 2007. Anti-racism's Dangerous Dinosaurs. *The National Post,* 20 November.

Kobayashi, A., and L. Peake. 2000. Racism Out of Place: Thoughts on Whiteness and an Anti-Racist Geography in the New Millennium. *Annals of the Association of American Geographers* 90 (2): 392–403.

Kukushkin, V. 2009. Immigrant-Friendly Communities: Making Immigration Work for Employers and Other Stakeholders. Ottawa: Conference Board of Canada.

Kulchynsy, P. 2009. The Emperor's Old Clothes. *Canadian Dimension*, 5 March. Available online.

Lawrence, B. 2004. *'Real' Indians and Others: Mixed-Blood Urban Native Peoples and Indigenous Nationhood*. Lincoln: University of Nebraska Press.

Lehr, J. 1991. Peopling the Prairies with Ukrainians. In *Canada's Ukrainians: Negotiating an Identity*, eds. L. Luciuk and S. Hryniuk. Toronto: University of Toronto Press.

Lewis, S. 1992. Report on Race Relations in Ontario. Toronto: Government of Ontario. Available online.

Li, P. 1994. Unneighbourly Houses or Unwelcome Chinese: The Social Construction of Race in the Battle over "Monster Homes" in Vancouver. *International Journal of Comparative Race and Ethnic Studies* 1 (1): 47–66.

——. 1998a. *The Chinese in Canada*. 2nd ed. Toronto: Oxford University Press.

———. 1998b. The Market Value and Social Value of Race. In *Racism and Social Inequality in Canada: Concepts, Controversies and Strategies of Resistance*, ed. V. Satzewich. 115–30. Toronto: Thompson Educational Publishing.

———. 2003. *Destination Canada: Immigration Debates and Issues*. Toronto: Oxford University Press.

Loney, M. 1998. *The Pursuit of Division: Race, Gender and Preferential Hiring in Canada*. Montreal and Kingston: McGill-Queen's University Press.

Makabe, T. 1981. The Theory of the Split Labour Market: A Comparison of the Japanese Experience in Brazil and Canada. *Social Forces* 59: 786–809.

Malešević, S. 2002. Rational Choice Theory and the Sociology of Ethnic Relations: A Critique. *Ethnic and Racial Studies* 25 (2): 193–212.

Manpower Services to Director General, Department of Manpower and Immigration. 1966. Memorandum. Library and Archives Canada. RG76. Volume 842. File 553–67, Part 3.

Marger, M. 1997. *Race and Ethnic Relations: American and Global Perspectives*. Belmont, CA: Wadsworth Publishing.

Matas, M. 2010. Robert Pickton's Sole Survivor Makes a New Life. *Globeandmail.com*, 14 August. Available online.

McIntosh, P. 1988. White Privilege and Male Privilege: A Personal Account of Coming to See Correspondences through Work in Women's Studies. Working Paper 189. Center for Research on Women, Wellsley College.

Melchers, R. 2006. Inequality before the Law: The Canadian Experience of "Racial Profiling." Ottawa: Royal Canadian Mounted Police. Available online.

Miki, R. 2005. *Redress: Inside the Japanese Canadian Call for Justice*. Vancouver: Raincoast Books.

Miles, R. 1982. *Racism and Migrant Labour*. London: Routledge & Kegan Paul.

———. 1993. *Racism after "Race Relations."* London: Routledge.

Miles, R., and M. Brown. 2003. *Racism*. 2nd ed. London: Routledge.

Miller, J. 1996. *Shingwauk's Vision: A History of Native Residential Schools*. Toronto: University of Toronto Press.

Mitchell, K. 2004. *Crossing the Neoliberal Line: Pacific Rim Migration and the Metropolis*. Philadelphia: Temple University Press.

Montagu, A. 1964. *Man's Most Dangerous Myth*. New York: World Publishing.

———. 1972. *Statement on Race: Annotated Elaboration and Exposition of the Four Statements on Race Issued by Unesco*. Oxford: Oxford University Press.

Mosher, C.J. 1998. *Discrimination and Denial: Systemic Racism in Ontario's Legal and Criminal Justice Systems, 1892–1961*. Toronto: University of Toronto Press.

Mujahid, A.M. 2009. A Profile of Muslims in Canada. Available online.

Nagler, M. 1975. *Natives Without a Home*. Toronto: Longmans.

Nakhaie, R. 2004. Who Controls Canadian Universities? Ethnoracial Origins of Canadian University Administrators and Faculty's Perception of Mistreatment. *Canadian Ethnic Studies* 36: 92–110.

Native Women's Association of Canada. 2010. What Their Stories Tell Us: Research Findings from the Sisters in Spirit Initiative. Ottawa: Native Women's Association of Canada.

Neu, D. and R. Therrien. 2003. *Accounting for Genocide: Canada's Bureaucratic Assault on Aboriginal People*. London: Zed Books.

Ontario Human Rights Commission. 2003. Paying the Price: The Human Cost of Racial Profiling. Toronto: Ontario Human Rights Commission.

Pew Research Center for People and the Press. 2009. Economy, Jobs Trump All Other Policy Priorities in 2009. *PeoplePress.org*, 22 January. Available online.

Policy Research Initiative. 2009. Understanding Canada's "3M" Reality in the 21st Century. Ottawa: Government of Canada.

Ponting, J.R., and J. Kiely. 1997. Disempowerment: "Justice", Racism, and Public Opinion. In *First Nations in Canada: Perspectives on Opportunity, Empowerment, and Self-Determination*, ed. J.R. Ponting. Whitby, ON: McGraw-Hill Ryerson.

Porter, J. 1965. *The Vertical Mosaic: An Analysis of Social Class and Power in Canada*. Toronto: University of Toronto Press.

Power, S. 1999. To Suffer By Comparison? *Daedalus* 128 (2): 31–66.

Pratt, A. 2005. *Securing Borders: Detention and Deportation in Canada*. Vancouver: University of British Columbia Press.

Preibisch, K. 2004. Migrant Agricultural Workers and Processes of Social Inclusion in Rural Canada: Encuentros and Desencuentros. *Canadian Journal of Latin American and Caribbean Studies* 29 (57–58): 203–239.

Quebec. 2008. Consultation Commission on Accommodation Practices Related to Cultural Differences. Building the Future: A Time for Reconciliation. Report by G. Bouchard and C. Taylor. Available online.

Rankin, J., et al. 2002. Singled Out: An Investigation into Race and Crime. *Toronto Star*, 18 October: A1.

Razack, S. 2008. *Casting Out: The Eviction of Muslims from Western Law and Politics*. Toronto: University of Toronto Press.

Rex, J. 1983. *Race Relations in Sociological Theory*. London: Routledge.

Richards, J. 2005. A Comment. In *Market Solutions for Native Poverty*, eds. H. Drost, B.L. Crowley, and R. Schwindt. Toronto: C.D. Howe Institute.

Roediger, D. 1991. *The Wages of Whiteness: Race and the Making of the American Working Class*. London: Verso.

Rolfsen, C., and M.F. Hill. 2009. Surrey Man Says Off-Duty Cops Robbed, Racially Abused Him. *Vancouversun.com*, 16 July. Available online.

Rosen, J., and C. Lane. 1995. The Sources of the Bell Curve. In *The Bell Curve Wars: Race, Intelligence and the Future of America*, ed. S. Fraser. New York: Basic Books.

Roy, P. 1989. *A White Man's Province: British Columbia Politicians and Chinese and Japanese Immigrants, 1858–1914.* Vancouver: University of British Columbia Press.

Royal Commission on Aboriginal Peoples. 1996a. Bridging the Cultural Divide: A Report on Aboriginal People and Criminal Justice in Canada. Ottawa: Supply and Services Canada.

———. 1996b. Report, Volume 1: Looking Forward, Looking Back. Ottawa: Supply and Services Canada.

Rushton, J.P. 1988. Race Differences in Behaviour: A Review and Evolutionary Analysis. *Personality and Individual Differences* 9: 1009–24.

Rushton, J.P., and A. Boegart. 1987. Race Differences in Sexual Behavior: Testing an Evolutionary Hypothesis. *Journal of Research in Personality* 21: 529–51.

Said, E.W. 1979. *Orientalism.* New York: Pantheon.

Satzewich, V. 1989. Racisms: The Reaction to Chinese Migrants in Canada at the Turn of the Century. *International Sociology* 4 (3): 311–27.

———. 1991. *Racism and the Incorporation of Foreign Labour: Farm Labour Migration to Canada since 1945.* London: Routledge.

———., ed. 1998a. *Racism and Social Inequality in Canada: Concepts, Controversies, and Strategies of Resistance.* Toronto: Thompson Educational Publishing.

———. 1998b. Race, Racism, and Racialization: Contested Concepts. In *Racism and Social Inequality in Canada: Concepts, Controversies and Strategies of Resistance*, ed. V. Satzewich. Toronto: Thompson Educational Publishing.

———. 2000. Whiteness Limited: Racialization and the Social Con-struction of "Peripheral Europeans." *Histoire sociale/Social History* 33 (66): 271–90.

Satzewich, V., and W. Shaffir. 2009. Racism Versus Professionalism: Claims and Counter-Claims about Racial Profiling. *Canadian Journal of Criminology and Criminal Justice* 51 (2): 199–227.

Schermerhorn, R. 1970. *Comparative Ethnic Relations: A Framework for Theory and Research.* New York: Random House.

Schissel, B., and T. Wotherspoon. 2003. *The Legacy of School for Aboriginal People: Education, Oppression and Emancipation.* Toronto: Oxford University Press.

Shepard, R.B. 1991. Plain Racism: The Reaction against Oklahoma Black Immigration to the Canadian Plains. In *Racism in Canada*, ed. O. McKague. Saskatoon: Fifth House Publishers.

Simmons, A. 1998. Racism and Immigration Policy. In *Racism and Social Inequality in Canada: Concepts, Controversies and Strategies of Resistance*, ed. V. Satzewich. Toronto: Thompson Educational Publishing.

———. 2010. *Immigration and Canada: Global and National Perspectives.* Toronto: Canadian Scholars Press.

Solomon, R.P., and H. Palmer. 2004. Schooling in Babylon, Babylon in

School: When Racial Profiling and Zero Tolerance Converge. *Canadian Journal of Educational Administration and Policy* 33: 1–16.

Solomos, J., and L. Back. 1995. Marxism, Racism and Ethnicity. *American Behavioral Scientist* 38: 407–20.

Special Committee on the Participation of Visible Minorities in Canadian Society. 1984. *Equality Now!* Ottawa: Minister of Supply and Services.

Standing Senate Committee on Human Rights. 2010. Reflecting the Changing Face of Canada: Employment Equity in the Federal Public Service. Ottawa: Senate of Canada. Available online.

Stasiulis, D., and A. Bakan. 2005. *Negotiating Citizenship: Migrant Women in Canada and the Global System*. Toronto: University of Toronto Press.

Statistics Canada. 2003. Ethnic Diversity Survey: Portrait of a Multicultural Society. Ottawa: Minister of Industry.

Steyn, M. 2006a. *American Alone: The End of the World as We Know It*. Washington: Regnery Publishing.

———. 2006b. The New World Order. *Maclean's Magazine*, 23 October.

Stormfront. 2009. The Accomplishments of the White Race. Available online.

Sugiman, P. 2006. Unmaking a Transnational Community: Japanese Canadian Families in Wartime Canada. In *Transnational Identities and Practices in Canada*, eds. V. Satzewich and L. Wong. Vancouver: University of British Columbia Press.

Sun Media. 2007. *Racial Tolerance Report*. January. Toronto: Leger Marketing.

Tanovich, D. 2005. *The Colour of Justice: Policing in Canada*. Toronto: Irwin Law.

Taylor, C. 1998/1999. On the Nisga'a Treaty. *BC Studies* 120 (Winter): 37–40.

Thatcher, R. 2004. *Fighting Firewater Fictions: Moving Beyond the Disease Model of Alcoholism in First Nations*. Toronto: University of Toronto Press.

Thompson, L. 1985. *The Political Mythology of Apartheid*. New Haven, CN: Yale University Press.

Titley, B. 1986. *A Narrow Vision: Duncan Campbell Scott and the Administration of Indian Affairs in Canada*. Vancouver: University of British Columbia Press.

Toronto Life. 2008. Girl, Interrupted. *Torontolife.com*, December. Available online.

Toronto Star. 2002. Fantino: We Do Not Do Racial Profiling. *Thestar.com*, 19 October. Available online.

Totten, M. 2009. Aboriginal Youth and Violent Gang Involvement in Canada: Quality Prevention Strategies. *IPC Review* 3 (March): 135–56.

Travis, H. 2006. Pickton Trial: Who Were the Victims? *TheTyee.ca*, 4 February. Available online.

Traynor, I. 2009. Swiss Ban the Building of New Minarets: Surprise Result, a Triumph for Far-Right Swiss People's Party, Likely to Enflame Muslim World. *Globe and Mail*, 30 November: A12.

Trumper, R., and L. Wong. 2007. Canada's Guest Workers: Racialized, Gendered, and Flexible. In *Race and Racism in 21st-Century Canada*, eds. S. Heir and B.S. Bolaria. Toronto: University of Toronto Press.

Ujimoto, V. 1988. Racism, Discrimination and Internment: Japanese in Canada. In *Racial Oppression in Canada*, eds. B.S. Bolaria and P. Li. Toronto: Garamond Press.

United Nations Development Program. 2009. *Human Development Report*. New York: United Nations Development Program. Available online.

van den Berghe, P. 1986. Ethnicity and the Sociobiology Debate. In *Theories of Race and Ethnic Relations*, eds. J. Rex and D. Mason. Cambridge: Cambridge University Press.

———. 1995. Does Race Matter? *Nations and Nationalism* 1 (3): 357–68.

von der Osten-Sacken, T., and T. Uwer. 2007. Is Female Genital Mutilation an Islamic Problem? *Middle East Quarterly* xiv (1): 29–36.

Ward, P. 2002. *White Canada Forever: Popular Attitudes and Public Policy towards Orientals in British Columbia*. 3rd ed. Montreal and Kingston: McGill-Queen's University Press.

Warry, W. 2008. *Ending Denial: Understanding Aboriginal Issues*. Toronto: University of Toronto Press.

Weinfeld, M. 2001. *Like Everyone Else … but Different: The Paradoxical Success of Canadian Jews*. Toronto: McClelland and Stewart.

Widdowson, F., and A. Howard. 2008. *Disrobing the Aboriginal Industry: The Deception Behind Indigenous Cultural Preservation*. Montreal and Kingston: McGill-Queen's University Press.

Wilson, D., and D. Macdonald. 2010. The Income Gap between Aboriginal Peoples and the Rest of Canada. Ottawa: Canadian Centre for Policy Alternatives.

Wilson, E.O. 1978. *On Human Nature*. New York: Vintage.

Windsor-Essex Economic Development Corporation. 2010. Leamington. *ChooseWindsorEssex.com*. Available online.

Winn, C. 1985. Affirmative Action and Visible Minorities: Eight Premises in Quest of Evidence. *Canadian Public Policy* 11 (4): 684–700.

Woodsworth, J.S. 1909 [1972]. *Strangers Within Our Gates: Or Coming Canadians*. Toronto: University of Toronto Press.

World Bank. 2006. *Expanding Job Opportunities for Pacific Islanders Through Labour Mobility at Home and Away*. New York: World Bank.

Wortley, S. 2005. Bias-Free Policing: The Kingston Data Collection Project, Preliminary Results. Toronto: Centre of Excellence for Research on Immigration and Settlement.

Wortley, S., and J. Tanner. 2003. Data, Denials and Confusion: The Racial Profiling Debate in Toronto. *Canadian Journal of Criminology and Criminal Justice* 45 (3): 1–9.

Zia, S. n.d. P.M. Condemns Hate Attacks. *Capital News Online*. Available online.

Index

Credits